SAPS FROM THE PINES

*A Collection of Stories
by Esther A. Rings*

www.trafford.com
North America & international
toll-free: 844-688-6899 (USA & Canada)
fax: 812 355 4082

I wish to dedicate this book to:

My mother, Anna Laura Hittle Rings, a saint if there ever was one, and to my eight siblings, their spouses and their children, who have loved me unconditionally, warts and all. My sister and brother-in-law, Marjorie and Robert Hamilton, have shared the mountains with me each summer since the cabin purchase, and other family members have gathered for reunions, celebrations, and ceremonies, creating memories more priceless than all the "gold in them thar hills."

This family photo was taken in 1928. We were a much happier bunch than this picture would lead you to believe.

Back row: Glen, Charles (Chuck), Marjorie (Marj), Helen, Clarence (Clancy), Earl
Front row: June, Arthur William,(father) Anna Laura,(mother) Esther, Robert (Bob)
Father, Arthur William, died in December, 1929, when I was three years old.

Family photo, 1956

Back row: Earl, Chuck, Glen, Clancy, Bob
Front row: Esther, June, Mom, Marj, Helen
Those still living in 2002: Marjorie (Marj), Robert (Bob), Esther

I also dedicate this book to Merla Kivett and her parents, Edna and Aldus Kivett. We purchased the cabin together in 1953, and they were responsible for most of the know-how when we renovated it in 1954. They are all three deceased, but my appreciation for them and our joint project increases with the years.

How many dedications are you allowed? I wish to include the names of two more people who have been long-term participants in the life of the cabin. Betty Campbell shared its joys and its upkeep from 1963 to 1981 and continues to make yearly visits. Niece Sally has been a part of the summer cabin scene since 1976 and loves that funny old place a much as I do.

In Appreciation

If I had the vocabulary of a scholar, I still couldn't adequately express my appreciation to my friends, Drs. Jane and Larry McGrath, for bringing this book into being. They have been my publishers, advisers, motivators, cheerleaders, and much more.

It all started when niece Sally and I invited the McGraths and Larry's sister and husband, Linda and Rich Wiggs, to the cabin for biscuits and sausage gravy. After dinner the conversation turned to the question of how I happened to acquire The Ol' Timer. That's always my cue to pull out my story of the purchasing and renovating of what was originally Jesse Williams' cabin, Snowcrest.

When I finished reading, Jane said, "Do you have any more stories?" and I said, "Oh, I have about eighteen skeleton chapters for a book I've been going to write, but they all need a lot of work." That's when they made this amazing offer. They said that if I'd polish those stories and add maybe a few more, they'd do whatever else it took to turn my writings into a finished product. They'd do the photo scanning, photo placing, computer "tech"-ing, pricing, detail tending, and any other grunt work involved in such a project. What a deal! Needless to say, I got moving.

Fortunately, Sally and I live just seven miles from the McGraths in Colorado in the summer and a few miles from them in Phoenix in the winter, and we've kept the paths hot between their homes and ours. They not only have all the know-how and skills needed for this undertaking, but they have amazed me with their enthusiasm, excitement, and patience every step of the way.

I was a little grumpy when I learned that they were taking a few weeks off for a tour of France. I offered to accompany them, thinking we could work as we traveled, but they muttered something about having other plans. (That's just a little joke I threw in so they don't get too uncomfortable with the praise.) Anyway, stars in your crowns, and gratitude more than I can express to you, Jane and Larry McGrath.

Special thanks also to my niece Dr. Sally Rings. She has been my skilled proofreader, a spelling and punctuation perfectionist of the first order. She is a stickler for a degree of accuracy that is not my style, but which certainly improves the quality of my writing.

In 1984, I took a leave of absence from my teaching job in Emporia, Kansas, and came to Arizona to work on my stories. Sally invited me to stay with her and her boys, David and Brian, for a year, and as she likes to tell people, she hasn't yet figured out how to get rid of me.

Sally has been most supportive of this project, letting me get by with a book absorption that leaves chores undone and schedules unmet. It took her a few weeks to figure out that her sabbatical project, due in May, was not as important as my April 15 book deadline, but now that she has that straight, things have been rolling along smoothly.

Thanks, Sally!

Gratitude and appreciation go also to friends Dr. Dosia Carlson and Greta Wiseman, who have critiqued my stories, helping me to clarify names, places, and situations which will not be familiar to many of my audience.

After Sally and I met Dosia in 1991, Dosia went home and told Greta she had found two more friends. Greta said, "We don't have room for any more friends." Sally and I persisted. Thanks, Dosia and Greta, for finding room for two more friends, and for supporting me so totally in my book writing.

To The Reader

This book has been in process over a span of forty-nine years. I've been able to document many details—names, places, dates, descriptions—through letters, photos, and newspaper clippings. In some cases, details have been recalled from memory and may not always be accurate, but they are true in essence.

Some stories, such as the first three chapters, were written in sequence, but many began as stand-alone vignettes. Those written as individual stories have, of necessity, repetition of descriptions, explanations, and details. There are so many people, places, and things introduced throughout the chapters of *Saps From The Pines,* that I hope the repetition is helpful in putting the pieces together, rather than distracting.

In selecting which events to include, I've considered my audience to be a mixture of family, friends, and those interested in Colorado history. Not all chapters will be of equal interest to this variety of readers, but my hope is that those of you who have the nerve to delve into this book after seeing the title and the cover photo will find some things that strike your fancy.

I invite reader response to these writings. Any additional information, corrections, or comments are welcome. You may write to:

Esther A. Rings
4114 E. Mercer Lane
Phoenix, Arizona 85028

FOREWORD

I got the first hint of my literary talents when I was in the fourth grade. Harold Haber, one of my classmates, lived on a farm outside our little town of Holton, Kansas, and our teacher, Miss Reed, decided we should take a field trip to the Habers to get acquainted with how our friends in the country made a living. Habers lived what seemed to me to be a great distance from town, and I was surprised to find that they had no next-door neighbors. With whom did Harold play? Play was certainly high on my list of activities, and how could you play without playmates? What's more, I was informed that farm children had chores to do after school and on weekends. I took a dim view of this.

When we returned to school, Miss Reed gave us an assignment. We were to write a story or poem describing our field trip observations. I chose to write a poem. I had heard the family mention that we were somehow related to the poet Robert Browning, Grandma Browning being a Browning and all. And so I wrote:

> *Today we went to Habers.*
> *They haven't any neighbors.*
> *They live so far away*
> *And work so hard all day.*

I don't remember how the poem was received by Miss Reed, but I knew it was worthy of the Browning name because family members would ask me to repeat it over and over. It must have made them happy to know that the poetry gene was alive and well in the DNA of little Esther Anna because they always laughed when I recited it.

That encouraged me to write a song in the fifth grade. I knew it was good because my teacher had me sing it at the PTA Columbus Day program.

If I were reading this story to you on a tape recorder, I could give you the tune, but since this is the printed version, you'll have to be satisfied with words only:

> *Columbus sailed the ocean blue*
> *In fourteen hundred ninety-two.*
> *He sailed and sailed across the sea*
> *And found this land for you and me.*

It was 1984 before I did any more serious writing. I had taken a leave of absence from my teaching job in Emporia, Kansas, to spend a year with niece Sally and write stories about summers at my cabin, The Ol' Timer. My writing went splendidly that first year, and I continued to add a story now and then until my retirement in 1990. Then things came to a halt. Retirement is a very busy time. I wouldn't recommend it for the lazy, the ailing, or for those inclined toward acedia. (I got that word from a Matthew Fox tape. Matthew says it means "lacking energy to begin new things." I've been looking for a place to use it.)

Now it is autumn, 2001, and I have decided this book needs to be ready for distribution at the Arthur and Anna Rings family reunion in July, 2002.

I wrote a different foreword some years ago. At the top I wrote, FORWARD. Spell check didn't catch it, but fortunately someone else did. I haven't been good at spelling or much of anything else since the first grade when I got all A's. My teacher, Miss Neibling, was our neighbor and a good friend of the family. Maybe some of my problem with spelling is because I have a tiny bit of "disleckseea,"* or perhaps it's because I learned the alphabet backwards in the first grade, or could it be my horizontal astigmatism? Whatever. As my sister Marj would say, "Close enough." Now that I think about it, it seems that FORWARD might have been the better word since the writing of this FOREWORD is definitely moving me FORWARD in this monumental task.

So, back to the computer to polish, edit, to delete, and add.

This will probably be the silliest book you've ever had.

Esther A. Rings

*I really know how to spell dyslexia; I just did that for fun.

Esther Rings and Harold Haber 6th Grade—
4th and 5th grade school photos were not available.

SAPS TERRITORY

N

GILPIN
PEAK TO PEAK HIGHWAY

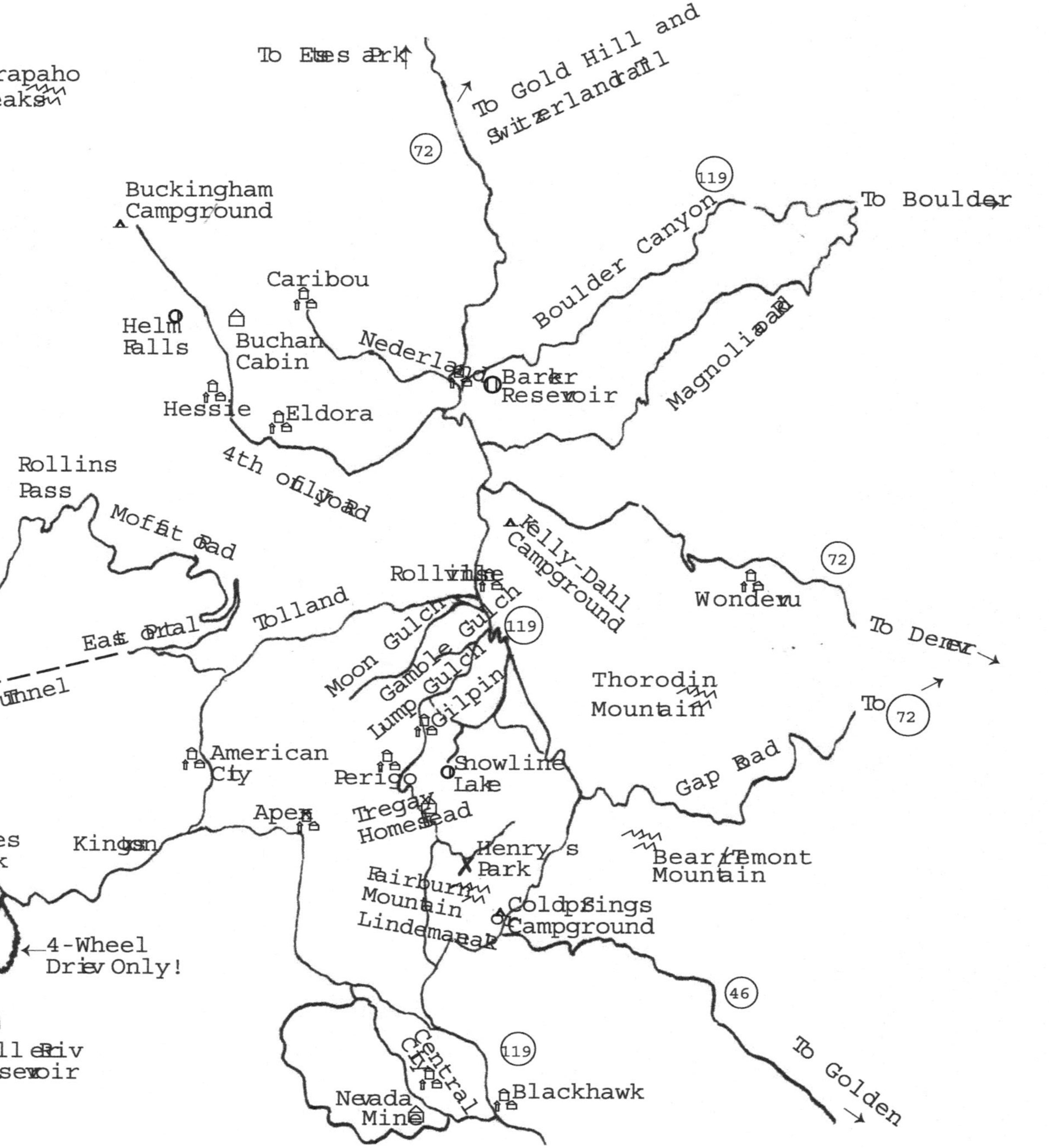

To Boulder

To Denver

72

72

To Golden

46

To Estes Park

To Gold Hill and Switzerland Trail

72

119

Magnolia Road

Boulder Canyon

Barker Reservoir

Nederland

Caribou

Buchanan Cabin

Eldora

Hessie

4th of July Road

Hell Falls

Buckingham Campground

Arapaho Peaks

Kelly-Dahl Campground

Wondervu

Thorodin Mountain

Gap Road

Beaver Mountain

Fremont Mountain

Coldsprings Campground

Lindemar

119

Central City

Nevada Mine

Blackhawk

Henry's

Airburn Mountain

Snowline Lake

Tregay Homestead

Perigo

Tumble Gulch

Gamble Gulch

Moon Gulch

Rollinsville

119

Tolland

Apex

American City

Kingston

James Peak

4-Wheel Drive Only!

Fall River Reservoir

Rollins Pass

Moffat Road

East Portal

Moffat Tunnel

Winter Park

CONTENTS

THE OL' TIMER
THROUGH THE SEASONS

1953
THE ADVENTURE BEGINS

"How would you like to join me in a summer adventure?" I asked my friend Merla over the phone. We had lived together in Council Grove, Kansas, during our first years of teaching and had stayed in touch when we went our separate ways. "Sounds great!" came her enthusiastic reply. "Do you have a plan?"

That's all it took to set the wheels in motion for a couple of "Saps" to take to the "Pines." The adventure we settled upon was to drive to the mountains of Colorado and find summer jobs. When school was out in May, we counted our pennies and figured we had enough to last about a week. By then we'd have the perfect jobs, and the money would start rolling in.

At the appointed time, I took a "milk train" from Topeka, Kansas, where I was visiting family. Merla was to meet me in the western Kansas town of Pratt, and from there we would drive in her vintage Ford, Beetlebomb, to Colorado and find ourselves an employment agency.

"Why is it called a milk train?" I asked my sister Marj and her husband Robert as they were depositing me at the Topeka train depot. I could always count on Robert for an answer, real or imagined. "You will find," says he, with his usual tone of authority, "that this conveyance will stop and milk every cow along the way."

"Ha, ha," says I.

He wasn't kidding. A letter home describes the trip:

> *Every time the train stopped I rose from my sprawled position and groaned. Finally the conductor came up and said, "What you need is a pillow," and went trotting back to his little storeroom. I was just imagining how fine it would be to have something soft under my head when he returned with a toilet paper box. "Better than nothing," he said, as he placed it where my head had been lopping. Well, it did help.*

The train pulled into the Pratt station at eight A.M. Merla had been waiting since four o'clock, so neither of us felt ready for a day of driving. We decided to return to her home in Haviland, Kansas, get some rest, and leave at two o'clock the next morning. The trip to Colorado was uneventful. We arrived at our destination travel-weary but full of excitement.

Our first attempt at job security was the employment office in Loveland, Colorado. "What did you have in mind?" asked the friendly voice behind the desk. "Well, we'd prefer something that's pleasant and lucrative, and in a beautiful setting." I answered with confidence. She suggested we try Estes Park. "Just think," I said to Merla as we started up Big Thompson Canyon, "a park is just the thing. Maybe we'll be park rangers, or hostesses, or something where all we have to do is be pleasant." I had taken on "pleasant" as one of my life goals ever since I'd seen the play, *Harvey*. A quote from that production had stayed with me. It went something like, "If you're going to make a go of life, you have to be 'oh so smart,' or 'oh so pleasant.'" No choice there. I'd take "pleasant."

The trip up the canyon offered beauty beyond our imaginations, but Estes Park? What a disappointment. "This isn't a park," I complained. "It's a town." We thought the altitude was too high and the place too touristy, so we stayed the night in a pretty little cabin by a stream and went to the employment office in Denver the next day. A card to my family tells what happened next:

> Guess what! By noon we had a job. Now sit down for the shock. We're television canvassers. We go from house to house getting appointments for the salesmen. It's really fun. We work four hours a day, five days a week and get twenty dollars a week plus ten dollars for every appointment that leads to a sale.

Disappointment number two. My next card home read,

> We stayed with the Denver job for two days and found it to be a big scam. We spent at least seven hours a day instead of four and were exposed to the most depressed sections of the city. We didn't want to encourage people who couldn't afford the basics to buy televisions.

By Saturday we were back at the Denver Employment Office. The lady who helped us said the only job she had for two women was in Evergreen in a nice eating house. The only catch was that they served drinks. Here we were, two young women from small, conservative towns in dry Kansas, having our first experience with the real world. What would our families and friends think about our serving drinks? But we were running low on money, and when the agent assured us that it was a respectable place, we went to Evergreen and got ourselves jobs as barmaids. We just couldn't pass up room and board, and twenty-four dollars a week, plus tips.

Our new place of business, Evergreen by the Lake, was well named. It was at the edge of an evergreen forest and overlooking Evergreen Lake. It seemed like a lovely spot to spend the summer. Our first shock came when we got a closer look at the cabin which was to be our home. It was picturesque from the outside, but inside it was dirty and musty smelling. I tried not to breathe. We wanted to leave, but since it was our only hope for free lodging, we told ourselves we could clean it and air it out and make it do.

On the following Monday afternoon we moved to Evergreen, unpacked, and moved into our less-than-desirable quarters. We ate our evening meal at the restaurant and studied the crowd. The bar was much busier than the dining tables. A few people got to feeling pretty high, and we got to feeling pretty low. We went to our living quarters to figure our finances and decided we'd have to earn a little money before we could move on. Mrs. Brewer, the manager, had casually mentioned that there would be an old man called "Hickey" sleeping in the cabin attic. "He's our janitor and handyman. The attic has its own entrance, so he won't bother you. You don't need to worry."

We went to the store, bought an Air Wick bottle, and back at the cabin we opened the windows, put sheets under us, housecoats and army blankets over us and fell into a deep sleep. In the middle of the night we were awakened by the sound of men's voices in our living room. I thought I'd have heart failure then and there. It sounded like one went into another bedroom and the second man left. Pretty soon we could hear someone walking around again. I grabbed a rubbing alcohol bottle and sat up in bed with my aim at the door. Finally it got quiet, and when I figured the intruder was asleep, I turned on the light and started packing. Merla, who was braver and more practical than I, said, "You know that our alternative is to sleep in the car." That didn't sound any better, and besides, with the light on it seemed less frightening. I said, "Okay then, you sleep next to the door." I gave her the bottle, moved to the other bed, turned out the light, and returned to my slumbers.

The next morning we learned that the intruder was the new dishwasher who was also to share our cabin for the summer. The boss admitted that he was a little strange but seemingly harmless. This was not going to work.

2

While Merla worked the day shift on Tuesday, I went to Denver to find another job. This time I was sent to Central City to Ye Olde Fashioned Eating House. Mert, the owner, asked if I'd ever done tray service. "Oh, yes," I said, "I did tray service when I worked my way through college." It was the truth. I had worked in the cafeteria at Bethany College in Lindsborg, Kansas. The students came through with their trays, and I served them. Mert said she'd let us know if she would need us.

I went back to Evergreen to work the night shift. I worked from five P.M. till two A.M. and had my first experiences as barmaid. I had never heard of such things as Singapore Slings and Moscow Mules, and I hadn't the foggiest idea how the barmaid system worked. I learned that I was to take orders for drinks from the customers, give my order to the bartender, pay the bartender with my own money, take the drinks to the customers, and collect my money.

That first night I took all of my one dollar bills, put them in my apron pocket, and headed for my first business transaction. Four young men sat down at one of my tables and ordered four beers. I got the four beers from the bartender, paid him a dollar from my pocket and got twenty cents change. I put the beers in front of my customers and gave them the twenty cents. They seemed very pleased, and that made me feel good. Before long they ordered four more beers and I repeated the operation, paid a dollar to the bartender, took the beers and the twenty cents change to the young men. They were getting more friendly with each round of beer. "This is fun," I thought as I returned to the bar for the fourth time. I reached into my pocket for another dollar and was startled to find that my funds were depleted. Panic struck as I realized that I had not only been buying the beers, but was tipping these young gentlemen as well. I will be eternally grateful for good clean American beer-drinking young men. When they saw my stricken countenance, they called me over, paid their bill, and gave me a generous tip. For the remainder of that week they were my best and most enjoyable customers. But they wouldn't let me forget how I had entertained them that first evening.

Thursday P.M. I got a call from Central City. Mert, the manager of Ye Olde Fashioned Eating House, was on the phone, "I've been thinking it over," she explained, "and I think I could use you and your friend to wait tables. Could you start next Wednesday?" We certainly could. Mert later became one of my best friends, and we had many good laughs over her reason for deciding to hire us. It was because of my previous experience with tray service. Mert wasn't fooled for long.

How shocked I was to learn what tray service really meant. The heavy oblong trays must have been 14 by 30 inches. Metal covers placed around and over the plates made it possible to stack them two deep so that there might be as many as six plates of food on one tray. You got down low, put one hand under the tray and the other hand at the tray's edge, and hoisted the things onto your shoulder. This job was definitely for young, healthy backs.

In Central City we rented a room from a lady we called Ma Griffith, or sometimes Griffie. She was a colorful character and we enjoyed her company, but getting from the restaurant to our room at her house was not easy. This is how I described it in a letter home:

> To give you an idea of how hilly Central City is, this is how we go home from work. We climb the first hill to the old Methodist Church, then turn right and climb the second hill. We turn left and make our way up the third hill which brings us to the steps in front of the Griffith house. We go up a flight of steps to their yard, up another flight to their porch, into the house and up another flight of stairs to the second floor and our bedroom. We look out our back window and see that we are on ground level.
>
> We live across the hall from the first violinist in the opera orchestra. He gets out his violin and practices his scales while we take our afternoon nap. The reason we have time for a mid-afternoon siesta is that we work from 10 A.M. to 2 P.M. and

5 P.M. till after the dinner rush. The lady in the next room plays the oboe. She has just now started practicing. So has the violinist. Someone else is playing the radio. I think I'll go take a walk. More later. Love, Esther

Later:

Have I told you about Hannah, our Swedish cook? Her cooking and baking can't be beat. People come from all over to eat her food. She and Mert, the boss, turn out fresh cinnamon rolls every morning, and hot rolls, cakes, and pies every meal. Her vegetable soup is out of this world. Kemmie is their assistant. She grows lovely flowers on the hill behind her home and keeps a fresh bouquet on each table. Mert and Hannah arrive at Ye Olde at about four A.M. each morning and start baking. By eleven o'clock, just before the noon rush, they are starting to sag, and can be found hiding behind the large refrigerator having a little nip of spirits in order to keep going.

Ye Olde Fashioned cooks, 1954—Hannah, Swedish cook; Kemmie, cook's helper and flower provider; Mert, boss and cook

Ye Olde Fashioned had an open kitchen. That meant that the customers could watch the cooks and the cooks could watch the waitresses to see that they did a good job. The dining area was divided into six stations, three tables each, with a waitress assigned to each. Every few days the waitresses were supposed to rotate to a new set of tables, as the ones in the front were the most popular and tipping was usually better.

New help always started at the stations closest to the kitchen where Mert and Hannah could keep a close tab on their progress. I don't know what all I must have done to displease, but when it was time to rotate, everyone got to move but me. I was retained for further observation. For several weeks I remained on what we came to call the "dunce station." Eventually I either caught on or they took pity on me, and I became one of the regular gang. We all celebrated.

Central City was an exciting place to work, and so was Ye Olde Fashioned since it was situated where much of the action took place. The historic Teller House hotel and the opera house across the street were attractions for tourists and opera goers. There were special days, such as the opening day of the opera season, when people

Ye Olde Fashioned open kitchen. Esther at dunce station.

dressed in old-fashioned costumes and paraded up and down the streets, enjoying the clowns, the German band, and the antique car show. Each day we could hear the opera cast practicing in a building nearby, or watch the square dancers who entertained the crowds before and after each opera performance. Bell ringers in old-fashioned costumes strolled up and down the streets announcing the scheduled events of the day. Many evenings, when the opera house wasn't full, the Ye Olde Fashioned crew was invited to attend the performances admission free, once our work was done.

4

During the first week of August, Merla's folks, Edna and Aldus Kivett, surprised us with a visit. The evening they arrived we left work as soon as possible, got in their car, and went in search of lodging for the four of us. We drove through the dark of night up highway 119 through Rollinsville, stopping at several cabins to inquire about lodging. There was nothing available that we could afford, so we started back to Central City, thinking that Merla and I would sleep on the floor and let Kivetts have our beds. Suddenly the car left the highway and headed down a small dirt side road. We thought Pop Kivett, the driver, had lost control. We didn't know that he had seen a sign which read, "BLUE SPRUCE, Cabins for Rent." What a find that was! George and Ruth Leyen were the owners of five log cabins beautifully situated at the bottom of the hill and at the edge of South Boulder Creek. George and Ruth were so friendly and the price so reasonable that we thought we had surely been led to this spot.

We all spent the night in cabin number two, dozing off to the sound of the mountain stream. The next morning we sat at breakfast enjoying the spectacular view of Arapaho Peak from our kitchen window. After breakfast we were visiting with Mr. Leyen. "Wouldn't it be great if we could have a cabin up in these mountains?" I jokingly remarked. George brightened. "I happen to have a log cabin for sale. Would you like to see it?" We thought it wouldn't cost anything to look, and we were in such an adventuresome mood, we said, "Sure." You can guess the rest.

When I wrote a birthday note to sister Marj, I told her I thought she'd like her birthday present.

Happy Birthday, Marj. I've just bought you part of a cabin. It cost me $125 for one-fourth interest in a four room cottage plus storeroom, outhouse, furniture, cooking utensils, the works. Of course, it's not in tip-top-shape, but it won't take

much to make a nice cozy place of it. There are two bedrooms plus a storage room which will accommodate three beds. That should handle several of us at a time. Wait till you see the yard. It has nicely terraced rock walls, hops vines growing up the side of the cabin, and gooseberry bushes all over the place. Two lakes are within walking distance. I'll tell you more when I see you.

Snowcrest (The Ol' Timer) at time of purchase, 1953.

I almost choke now when I read the part about it not taking much "to make a nice cozy place of it." We were so excited about our purchase that we had to show it off. We had a big picnic in the side yard of the cabin and invited all of the Central City gang. Then we gave a tour through the cabin. Boss Mert told me later that she went home feeling sick about what we had done. She was sure there was no way that such a tumbled down shack could ever be made livable, not even as a rustic vacation getaway.

I'll save the details of what it was really like for the next chapter. It is enough to say that we returned to our Kansas teaching jobs full of plans and excitement, and in anticipation of summer 1954, when we would "cozy up" the place.

THE ADVENTURE BEGINS

Blue Spruce cabins with Big Dutch mountain in background

Esther and Merla in Ye Olde Fashioned waitress dresses

Opening day of the opera in Central City - Clowns

Central City bell ringer announcing opera, tours, and other events of interest

Central City gang enjoying a picnic in side yard of The Ol' Timer, 1954

Opening day of the opera in Central City – German band

7

COZYING UP THE PLACE

Before leaving for Colorado on that first summer of adventure in 1953, I had been offered a job in a rural community near El Dorado, Kansas, where Merla was teaching. She had invited me to live with her and drive the seventeen miles to Leon where I would teach music, grades one through high school. I had accepted both offers. Therefore, when we returned from Colorado after that first exciting summer of adventure, I moved to El Dorado to share a little yellow bungalow with Merla. We spent much time that winter visiting with her parents and planning our strategy for fixing up our newly-acquired mountain cabin. Merla's father Aldus was a jack-of-all-trades. After serving for a number of years as a minister in Quaker communities, he had retired to a hobby of renovating old houses. He and his wife Edna would buy a place that was about to fall down, and together they'd turn it into a nice piece of rental property. Therefore, they were the brawn and the brains of our cabin project. Throughout the winter they acquired many materials which, if we could get them to Colorado, would save us time and money. They had even decided that we should have a chicken house and chickens in order to save on the food bill.

Aldus and Edna Kivett, the brawn and brains of the cabin renovation

My first 1954 postcard from Colorado to my family looked like it had been through the war. It was dated June 5 and began, *"If you think this card has taken a beating, you should see me."*

Part of the beating had happened on the trip through Western Kansas. Not that it hadn't been fun and exciting, but it HAD taken its toll. A letter written June 13 is a reminder of that wild trip:

Kiv took the lead in her parents' car and kept us on the right road. Pop Kivett came next in the loaded pickup, and I, in Merla's car, was assigned rear gunner to watch the load. Every time the tarp came loose or something would slip, I'd swing out and blink my lights, and the whole caravan would stop at the side of the road. We'd all jump out and pull and tug till everything was in place again. This happened quite often due to an encounter with a Western Kansas dust storm. The only consolation was that it helped keep us awake and gave us a chance to stretch and visit.

The truck was loaded something like this: The sides of the chicken house stood on either side of the truck bed and came well above the cab. Packed between these extensions were the following: washing machine, cement mixer, bed, springs, two mattresses, large glass window, screen door, power mower, garden tools, Pop's tool chest, Morris chair, rocking chair, and two crates of chickens, besides little things I can't remember now. It was some fun getting that caravan through Denver. The chickens were frightened half to death. They stacked up on top of each other and feathers went flying everywhere. There were expressions of utter disbelief on the faces of people who passed or met us as we made our way along Colfax Avenue in the heart of downtown Denver during rush hour traffic.

When our caravan pulled into Blue Spruce at about eight P.M., there had been a snow storm the day before and the temperature was sixteen degrees. George and Ruth Leyen weren't at home, but we were too tired and cold to wait for their return. We simply dragged our weary bodies into friendly cabin number two and went to bed. George said they were quite surprised when they arrived home and found they had been invaded. I wonder now how those chickens ever survived the trip and the cold night.

We were up early the next morning, and after a hurried breakfast we drove the two miles to our purchase of the previous summer. Pop went to work on the chicken house while Merla, her Mom, and I removed junk and burned trash. By seven P.M. we'd hardly made a dent. The most we could say for the day was that the chickens had a home. As for us, we returned to Blue Spruce for the night.

The next morning we went to Denver for materials. That took most of the day, and I'd have been ready to call it quits. But Kivetts were used to working long hours, so we came back to the cabin and cleaned some more.

Saturday Pop and I covered the back roof. That's the part over the bunk house, storage room, and kitchen. We used green roll roofing and stuck it down with tar. By that night I looked like a real tar baby. We must have done a fairly good job, in spite of the fact that we laid the strips vertically rather than horizontally and we didn't overlap them. Thirty-seven years later we still had the same roof, though I must admit, it had undergone many a patch job.

Pop Kivett, Esther, and Merla roofing the back of the cabin

This might be a good time to describe this "cozy little place" as it really was. It is true that from the outside it was picturesque, in an old, run-down cabin sort of way. The hops vines climbing the outside logs, the terracing, and the gooseberry bushes did give it a certain rustic charm. Then there was the inside. A path led up the east side of the house to the kitchen door. This became our main entrance since the living room floor was buckled, keeping the front door from opening very wide.

Esther at the kitchen door of Snowcrest (The Ol' Timer)

It was obvious that the first room we entered was the kitchen as it had the old Buck's Range, a wood-burning cook stove. The only other furniture was a sad-looking kitchen table, which we still use. The ceiling was a heavy cardboard material , sagging miserably from much rain, snow, and leaky roof. Suspended from this beat-up ceiling was a fairly modern-looking fluorescent light. It seemed inconsistent that this old place had been wired for electricity, but we were grateful.

The inside walls were wide, rough, unpainted boards, with quarter- to half-inch cracks between, and the linoleum had lost most of its pattern. There were no cupboards, just a big, bare room with a small opening into what is now our dining room, but at the time it appeared to have been used as a bedroom.

This bedroom/dining room had two narrow windows and a small door into the next room, so that it was very dark. The ceiling was similar to that in the kitchen, except that the sagging was worse. The walls of the dining room as well as the rest of the cabin were log, and where the chinking was missing, there had been many creative attempts at closing the gaps. Between the logs we found rolled up papers, rags, gunny sacks, and bits of fur. Over some of the logs were flattened cardboard boxes nailed in place with one-inch circular nail head protectors. These were a challenge to remove. The floor was rough, warped board, partly covered with another worn linoleum, and a trap door next to the living room wall led to a dirt cave below.

The living room ceiling was a gunny sack material which had collected dirt over the years, giving it a "swoop" effect. The morning Pop announced that it was time to remove that dirty over-hang was the day the rest of us decided we needed to go to town.

There was a half partition between the living room and what is now our front bedroom. Many of the logs in these rooms had been whitewashed. This was another fun removal job. These front rooms were where we found most of our treasures, though they didn't look so valuable at the time. There was an alabaster lighthouse which now sits in the dining room window, an old wind-up phonograph, a glass-front bookcase and a library table, a dining room table and chairs, a cigar lighter and Old Drum, a very large whiskey bottle. Somewhere in one of the three front rooms was a huge cherry-wood bed, which we eventually discarded, and the bunk beds which we still use in the back bedroom. The antlers which hang on the living room wall were found among the other treasures.

Two of the back rooms had dirt floors and were piled with junk. Next to the door into the kitchen was the funniest refrigerator I'd ever seen. It had to have been homemade and was so big that when we decided to get rid of it, we had to dismantle the thing to get it out the cabin door. It did work, however, if you could remember to plug it in and unplug it every few hours. We actually used it for a short time. The nights were so cold that we could unplug it before we went to bed, and old frig would stay cold till morning. There were a couple of large wooden crates in one of the rooms, and Pop, being both handy and thrifty, saw that they would make good kitchen cabinets. Those are the same cabinets we use today.

In one of my letters I described some of the fix-up process:

We spent every free minute getting the layers of paper and cardboard off the logs and preparing them for re-chinking. That included the removal of the white-wash. Once that was done we cut strips of metal lathe to put between all the cracks to hold the chinking. That was hard work and so was the chinking. We got the mixture all over the logs and had to remove it with a brush on a rotary drill. When that was done we sprayed the logs with a clear finish that made them look clean and shiny. That was the fun part.

While we were doing this, Pop was taking down the ceilings and putting up new rafters. Then came my least favorite job, putting up the sheet rock ceilings. Do you know how heavy sheet rock is? That's something I will surely never forget. There is a neat little gadget that most people use when putting up such ceilings. It's called a dummy, and is a couple of boards shaped like a T. One person standing on the floor holds the sheet rock in place with this marvelous invention while another person, perched on a ladder, nails it to the rafters. You must already have the pic-ture. We didn't have a wooden dummy, but we had a makeshift dummy. It was ME! I would stand on a table, bend my head forward so that the sheet rock would rest on my shoulders and arms, and Pop would go whomp, whomp, whomp, with his hammer and nails. The large bone at the back of my neck is starting to ache as I write this.

Other jobs included putting down mopboards, enlarging the two windows and openings in the dining room to let in more light, pouring cement floors in the back rooms, building the kitchen cabinets, putting linoleum coverings on the dining room and living room floors, and painting all the woodwork. Covering those warped, sloping floors took some creativity. It was not enough to layer the bare wood with tarpaper. More padding was needed. Why not use stacks of newspapers? After all, they were in bountiful supply. When I say stacks, I mean stacks. The thick layers of the daily news sheet not only protected the linoleum but also added a definite bounce to each step.

In addition to all this manual labor, we had to take time for frequent trips to Denver and Boulder for supplies. Our total expenditures for these necessities came to $500 for the summer.

Quoting another letter:

It probably sounds like we're poor planners as often as we have to go to town, but you should see that pickup sag every time we head for home. I didn't know building materials weighed so much.

Monday it was too cold to work up here, so we loaded our old dirty mattresses into the truck and went to Denver again. They have a place where they re-process mattresses so they're good as new. We got three full-size, two singles for the bunk beds, and two pillows for $45. We were looking for used studio couches for our living room, and to use for beds. They were all so dirty and rough looking that we were about to give up when we saw a green leather studio and platform rocker set with blonde wooden arms. Seventy-five dollars was more than we wanted to pay, but they looked so clean and sturdy, we just up and bought them. They're beautiful, and will be so practical for the cabin. We also got a nice oak chest of drawers which we have varnished and use for linens.

The other day in Central, we bought a little heating stove to put in our living room. It's called an Estate Oak and has a cameo picture on the front. It's cozy and old fashioned and will do till we have time and money for a fireplace. It cost $10."

My last big job at the cabin before the opera season began, and we went in to Central City to work for Mert, was shingling the rest of the roof.

The following is from another letter to family:

Wednesday I learned how to shingle. We picked out a green and silver color asphalt shingle and it looks great, what we have done. Pop worked with me one afternoon, and then I worked the next morning by myself. I wore out two pair of jeans and part of my seat. Maybe that's why they call them "thick-butt" shingles.

Last night I took a look in the mirror when the day's work was done and decided that even my mother wouldn't claim me. My hair hadn't been washed or put up for two weeks, and I hadn't had a bath in a week. We try to clean up before we go to town, but as you can imagine, we still look like hicks. It doesn't help any that we have to go through the aspen grove to the spring to haul all of our water.

We finally couldn't stand it any longer. After we had scrubbed all the floors and straightened the house, we got out the vitreous china bowl, another of our cabin finds, washed hair and took baths. We put the bowl on the floor in front of the kitchen range to wash our feet, and it reminded me of Saturday nights when I was a kid and we all took our baths in the galvanized tub. When we were clean from head to toe, we sat and drank hot tea in front of the open oven door and listened to pretty music on the radio. When I went to bed, I looked out the window and saw the moon coming up over the mountain. I took a deep contented breath. This surely must be living at its best.

COZYING UP THE PLACE

The green vinyl couch with blond arms, purchased in 1954, is still in use in 2002.

Buck's Range was in the kitchen at time of purchase. These rolls were not baked in Buck's oven, but it makes a pretty picture.

The wind-up phonograph was in the cabin at time of purchase.

Estate Oak stove, a $10 purchase in 1954

The antique bookcase and the square cigar lighter on top were among the treasures found in the cabin.

The moon shone over the mountain. This surely was "living at its best."

15

LIVING AT ITS BEST

In that first summer of our "very own cabin" and our "very own mountains," there were many experiences that caused us to exclaim, "This is living at its best." One was the delight we found in the bird and animal friends that shared our yard and, in the beginning, our house. After we thought we had all the small entrances closed, I awakened one morning to find a full-grown ground squirrel standing on hind legs in the middle of the bedroom floor. "Get a load of this!" I hollered to Merla. She came running from the kitchen where she'd been cooking bacon over the old Buck's Range, our wood-burning cook stove. "Well, look who's ready for breakfast!" she exclaimed.

That was all very cute, but when I reached into a sack of groceries and a chipmunk jumped out at me, that was a little much. We did another search for cracks or holes that might give them access to our larder. We loved feeding the creatures but preferred being in charge of where, what, and when. We were fascinated with the amounts of nuts and grain they could stuff into their pouches

Ground squirrel Lola was especially greedy. We named her after the song, "Whatever Lola Wants, Lola Gets." She ruled the stoop to our kitchen door and would stand at the screen each morning waiting for her handout. She was a veritable vacuum cleaner and could sweep up a pile of grain faster than we could deliver. But she especially delighted in peanuts. Once she had skillfully removed the shells, she would poke the nuts into her jaws till she appeared to have a bad case of two-sided mumps. Undaunted by lack of space, she would try for one more peanut. She'd poke it into one protruding jaw and it would pop out. She'd try the other jaw. No luck. Then she'd turn it around in her paws and try it from a different angle. Out again. Next she'd peel off the thin brown layer of skin. Still no success. The final attempt would be to break the nut into two pieces. If that didn't work, she would give up, dash to her hole, empty her aching jaws with amazing speed, and return to her pantry before we had time to lavish too much attention on her rivals.

Down the road from us, "by de dump road where you see de sign vot's got no writin' on it," lived an old miner named John El Gaddis. He'd drive past our place on the way to the War Eagle Mine where he still dug and dreamed of riches. If we were in the yard he'd stop to chat. One day when he was watching us feed our greedy creatures, he said, "Dem chipmunks gonna get so fat dey'll haf to vare girdles to get in dere holes."

The yard was always alive with activity. Mountain bluebirds flitted from their home on the telephone pole to the electric wires in front of the house, to the roof of the outhouse, and sometimes to the window where they would try to court the reflection of themselves in the glass. The wrens who lived in abandoned woodpecker holes in the aspen grove were fond of our woodpile. It must have housed a wealth of insects and bugs. These feisty little birds objected to our use of the yard and scolded mightily, with upturned tails fanning the air in indignation. The Steller's Jays had dispositions as cranky as their looks. If we tried to have our own breakfasts before we had tended to these feathered friends, their raucous calls reminded us to re-evaluate our priorities. A family of rabbits lived in the gooseberry bushes just outside the dining room window. Little did they know what a great view we had of their hiding place as we sat in our chairs in the corner of the dining room, sipping a last cup of tea before the day lured us into activity.

"That was a close one!" exclaimed Merla one day as she came in from feeding the critters. "I just got bombed by a hummingbird. I thought that beak was going right through my nose."

"We'd better feed the poor thing," I suggested, and after our next trip to town we had a sugar water feeder hanging from a hook over the kitchen window. It didn't take long for news to spread through the broadtail community that a new food source was available, and soon we were overtaken with dive, dart and drink. It was fun to watch the constant scramble for a position on one of the four perches. An air traffic controller would have been helpful.

Bathing and dishwashing became desirable activities as they offered acceptable excuses for watching the hummingbird show without being accused of time-wasting. By midsummer the bath accommodations had been improved due to the purchase of an oblong, galvanized tub. What a luxury it was to stretch out in that container of hot water in front of the well-stoked kitchen range and soak away sore muscles. To have it topped off with the sight and sound of a dozen or so hummingbirds framed by the kitchen window was the ultimate treat.

One morning in mid-July as I was standing at the kitchen sink, hands in dishwater, gazing out the window at the wonders before me, I felt compelled to stop and record the variety of nature's gifts I was privileged to see. Drying my hands, I took scratch paper and pencil and scribbled:

DISHWASHING AT THE CABIN

How can you mind doing dishes at the cabin when:
   the window over your kitchen sink looks out onto quaking aspen, lodge-
   pole pine, clear blue sky and fluffy clouds?

How can you mind doing dishes at the cabin when:
   you can feast your eyes on a garden of gaillardia, penstemon, loco,
   bedstraw, yarrow, cinquefoil, mariposa, and wild rose, and you didn't lift
   a finger or bend a back to help it bloom?

How can you mind doing dishes at the cabin when:
   nuthatch takes possession of the peanut butter mix on the old leaning
   pine tree, pine sisken sits at your new feeder and nibbles dainty bites of
   sunflower seed, and chickaree squirrel brings her babies to the feeder in
   the Colorado spruce?

How can you mind doing dishes at the cabin when:
   baby ground squirrels frolic over each other, luxuriating in dirt baths up
   the path, and young bunny explores his unlimited salad bar?

How can you mind doing dishes at the cabin when:
   broadtail hummer zooms in from outer space to have a sip from the
   sugar water feeder hung at eye level just outside the window and he's so
   close you can see him breathing; when delicately designed black and
   yellow butterfly flits from blossom to blossom tasting nectar as a wine
   taster tests aged wines.

All of these gifts of nature have been mine to enjoy in this brief time I've stood at the kitchen sink, hands in hot soapy water, passing dishes from suds to rinse to drainer.

Do I look at my dishes?

Do I see that they are sparkling clean?

Is it important?

Do I mind doing dishes at the cabin?

Bring on the pots and pans. Here comes a red-shafted flicker.

Another of our joys that first cabin summer, 1954, was our new friend and neighbor, Jim Murray. We had met him the summer before, but there hadn't been time to get acquainted. I described him in one of my letters:

Our neighbor Jim Murray is quite a character. He's past eighty years old but still roams the hills looking for gold. He wishes we could buy the land in back of us as he knows where there's a good vein of gold. He says he'll show us where it is, but he won't let anyone else in on his secret. He's become a self-appointed guardian of our property. Says he came over every evening last winter to see that everything was O.K. He even got up on the roof and fastened down some loose shingles. He writes poetry and songs and plays the guitar. His wife died in the early forties and he built his house up here shortly after that. I think he's glad to have some activity around here. I hope we'll have more time to enjoy him before the summer is over.

We did have time to enjoy Jim that summer. He invited each of our guests to tour his home and was glad to give a little local history to anyone who had time to listen. By the time we left for Kansas that fall, we had adopted each other as extended family members. The chapter "Prospector Jim" gives more of Jim's story.

As I mentioned earlier, working at Ye Olde Fashioned Eating House was fun. We had a great gang of workers. The crew was mostly made up of owner Mert's family: Mary Mattivi, Mert's daughter-in-law, was the hostess and bookkeeper. Mert's daughter Shirley, Mert's sister Emma, and Emma's daughter Kate were all waitresses. Those of us who were not family were graciously admitted to the inner circle. Besides Merla and me, there were Jo, a seasoned waitress, who took her job more seriously than the rest of us, and Bill, the dishwasher, who was not cut out for the fast pace of Mert's establishment. Closing time would usually find him far behind in his work and on the brink of panic. The rest of us would pitch in and sling dishes in ways that must have made Mert more than a little nervous. As we swept the floors and got things ready for the next day, we'd sing at the top of our voices, such songs as "I've Been Workin' on the Railroad," "You are my Sunshine," "Clementine," oldies that we all knew. Mary, sitting in a back room tending to her bookkeeping, admitted later that it was very hard to concentrate, given all the horseplay that was going on out front.

Besides the gang we worked with, there was the group of local "intimates," the daily customers. These included Earl Quiller and Morgan Gray, who together ran the only grocery store in town. Mert bought all of her supplies through them, so they came each morning for one of her delicious cinnamon rolls and a cup of coffee, as well as to get the grocery order. Mert bought the best of everything. She demanded quality and they delivered. George and Maryanne Springer ran the drugstore next door and came in most days for lunch and a little local news swapping. Mert's son and Mary's husband, Don Mattivi, a great tease, always added to the mayhem. There was "Fats" Grenfell, the County

Commissioner, who managed to get us some fancy signs pointing the way to the old Gilpin townsite. These were a great help in guiding family and friends to the cabin. Ray Laird was another regular customer. He was editor of the *Central City Register Call*, a newspaper which dated back to the mining days. All of these people and their families became our Central City social circle. We had a couple of big get-togethers that first summer and each succeeding summer that we worked at Mert's. The events were often held at the cabin. The *Register Call* carried a fun-poking account of one of these picnics in its column, "Upcoming Social Events."

> The two glamorous school teachers from Kansas who have been assimilating psychology and knowledge of the human race as waitresses at Ye Olde Fashioned Eating House, in order they may more aptly expound to their pupils when they return to their curriculum duties as to the way of life, extend an invitation to all citizens of Gilpin County to join with them in a momentous occasion at their cabin at Gilpin, Colorado, Monday evening, August 15th, where they have prepared two dozen weiners, a half watermelon and two small packages of potato chips to appease the hunger of those who attend, These two school marms, Misses Merla Kivett and Esther Rings recently purchased a cabin at Gilpin, which is over fifty years of age, has been named "The Old Timer," have made many improvements thereon and now is comparable to their beauty. Nothing but H20 will be served as both femmes are strict adherents of the W.C.T.U. tenets. It is anticipated that a wonderful and pleasant evening will be enjoyed.

I doubt that Ray Laird would have wished to claim this literary jewel. We never did know who had submitted it or how it passed the inspection of the editor. The account was accurate in that a pleasant evening was enjoyed by all.

One of the most exciting things for me that first summer was a week in August when I was able to share the cabin, the mountains, and my new friends with my family. My letters home that summer were full of plans and anticipation.

> *We can arrange to sleep thirteen here easily and we have plenty of floor space for extra cots and floor beds, so get everyone planning on that second week in August.*

It had never taken much coaxing to get my family interested in assembling. Brother-in-law Robert always said that the mere mention of food and fun was all it took to bring the tribe together. I hadn't stopped to consider the strain that fifteen or twenty people might put on our three-holer, or how many buckets of water would be needed for cooking, cleaning, dishes, and drinking. Our water source was Jim's spring, a "fer piece"' down the road, or through the aspen grove.

In re-reading my sister Marj's log about their first cabin trip, I find mention of nineteen people at the cabin that week. Fifteen were there most of the time, and the other four were drop-ins. I don't know how many she might have neglected to mention. It showed good judgment on the part of Merla's folks that they felt called to return to Kansas before the Rings tribe descended.

According to the log, Marj and Robert brought daughters, Carol and Janet, and Mom in their car. In addition to luggage for the five of them, they brought blankets, pillows, and miscellaneous cabin furnishings. Caravaning with them from Kansas were brother Glen, his wife Nell, and their two children, Dale and Jeannie, plus their week's worth of paraphernalia. From Iowa came sister June, husband Chic, and their two boys, Roger and John. At varying times through the week we were visited by my college friends, Ken and Irene Shaw, and family friends, Galen and Ula Ewing. Sister Helen, her husband Ivan, and their children, Geneva, Charles, and Joan, had dropped by earlier but must have sensed the inevitable confusion and had moved on.

Somehow Merla and I managed to mix work and play that week and were able to show the crowd some of our favorite haunts. Besides having Monday off, we drove to the cabin after work several nights and had a little morning time for short hikes and drives before returning to Ye Olde Fashioned in time to serve lunch. During breaks between the lunch and dinner shifts, we treated our guests to the exciting activities and interesting history of Central City. I was surprised to find the following entry in my journal describing that week.

> *One night after work we drove to the cabin to find everyone in bed and asleep.*
> *We got out bucket and brush and proceeded to paint the kitchen cabinets.*

As I look back on that first summer of showing off "our very own cabin" and "our very own mountains," I'm reminded of a quote from the book, *I Touch The Earth, The Earth Touches Me*, by Hugh Prather:

> *Ted "Bull" Howard races his jeep up and down his ranch trying to convince*
> *himself that he owns it. Maybe some day he will notice those billion-year moun-*
> *tains laughing at him.*

Surely that sixty-year-old cabin and those billion-year-old mountains, Arapaho, Thorodin, and Lindeman, had a good laugh that summer. And the joke's not over yet as I continue to share with family and friends what I consider to be "living at its best."

LIVING AT ITS BEST

War Eagle Mine in the hills above Gilpin, where John El Gaddis was going to strike it rich

Nuthatch at the suet feeder by the kitchen door

Broadtail hummingbirds feeding outside the kitchen window at The Ol' Timer

Columbine and gaillardia growing in the back yard

Golden Mantled Ground Squirrel, Lola, ready for breakfast at The Ol' Timer

23

GIVING UP THE GHOST

"Where is this cabin of yours?" someone might ask politely after hearing one of my soliloquies on summers in Colorado.

My favorite response would be, "It's in the ghost town of Gilpin, up Lump Gulch." Which isn't exactly true any more. Not the "ghost town" part. The abandoned town site of Gilpin began giving up its ghostly appearance shortly after we took possession of the Lump Gulch cabin.

I had liked the idea of living in a ghost town. It sounded pioneer and rustic, quaint and simple, and back-to-nature. Which is what it was in those early days.

There could have been little quarrel with the term "ghost town" in the late summer of 1953 when George Leyen first showed us what was to become "our very own cabin." George did point out that there were a few permanent or summer residents in the area. Bill Rosner was living in the old boarding house, caretaking the property for the owner, Mrs. Daugherty. There was Jim Murray, who was to become our good friend and neighbor, and Merrill Slater, who was renovating a log cabin nestled in the lodgepole pines behind Jim's place. Around the bend and out of sight of the town proper was a two-story frame house, a barn, and some wire pens, the remains of an old fox farm. A cowboy singer by the name of Ozie Waters was staying there part-time, though he had a job with a radio station in Denver. Across from the boarding house, east of Jim's place, were three very run-down structures. Two were one-room log cabins and the other was a small gray frame building. It was obvious that they belonged to a much earlier time.

A prize winning fox at the fox farm. Photo 1927

There were other cabins or buildings off the main road that didn't appear to be in use. The town seemed pretty ghostly to us. In fact, there was so little activity in the gulch in those first weeks when we were working on the cabin that whenever a car came up the road, we'd say, "Looks like we're getting company," and we usually were.

By mid-June of 1954, as we were "cozying up the place," we began to see signs of change. A bulldozer was unloaded from a truck one day, and it and its operator began making new roads to the west and north of our cabin. Then began a procession of vehicles. Each day truckloads of lumber and other items passed through town, turned the corner and disappeared in the direction of the fox farm.

Jeanne McKinstry feeding a calf at the fox farm (originally the Tregay homestead). Aluminum beaver fence in the background. Photo, 1928.

We were to learn that the property known locally as the old Tregay homestead, which included the fox farm, had been purchased by a Dr. J. M. Newman. He and his son Ward, with the help of the cowboy singer Ozie Waters, were developing an outdoor recreation camp in the upper meadow. It was to include a fort, a fishing pond and an area for a dramatic re-enactment of frontier days with Indian attacks on covered wagon caravans, etc. The camp was to be called Fort Cody.

We, the Kivetts and I, felt it our duty to keep an eye on the progress of this apparition as it became reality. We watched as a fine fort took shape, complete with lookout tower and sturdy gates. Within the inside walls, booths were set up to house souvenir and concession stands. Huge commercial refrigerators and freezers were hauled up the mountain and placed in some of the booths so that food could be stored and sold. A stage was constructed with a floor of rough lumber. An upright piano took its place at the side of the stage. In the center of the entire structure was a fire pit circled with benches. We could imagine that there would be singing and guitar strumming around the campfire with star-filled skies and moonlit nights.

Captain Ozie Waters, cowboy singer who had The Little Rangers program. Left, Betty Ann Huntsman Palmer. Right, Gloria Waters and Dickie Huntsman. Early stages of Fort Cody in background. Betty Ann and Dickie were great-grandchildren of Tregays. Photo, 1954.

Across the road from the fort was a grassy slope which was to be the site of the Indian massacres. Covered wagons appeared, and Indian teepees. A fishing pond was dug in a clearing surrounded by pine and aspen trees. It was fed by the Lump Gulch stream, former home and playground of many beaver.

Two cast members from the D'Oyle Carte Opera Company performing in Central City spent a day at The Ol' Timer. We took them to see Fort Cody. Max, Lilyon and Esther

Lilyon, Merla and Max

Ozie Waters had the perfect advertising channel to promote this operation. He was interested in young people, and his radio show featured a club for young listeners, the Little Rangers Club. One could become a member and receive a Little Rangers badge by writing to Ozie in care of the radio station.

It must have been early July when Indians imported from Idaho moved into their tents on the side of the hill and the action began. Carloads of families drove past the cabin, or stopped to inquire, "Is this the road to Fort Cody?" Signs had been placed at strategic intersections, but by the time people had driven a couple of miles on the narrow dirt road, some were certain they were lost.

There were probably a number of reasons why Fort Cody did not survive the summer. Rumor had it that the financial backers ran out of money and that the Indians were eating up the profits. It may have been that their advertising was premature, and that the Little Rangers and their families arrived before the activities were fully organized. Or perhaps the accommodations were just too primitive. Often a carload of people who had stopped at the cabin for directions to the fort was seen a short time later heading back to the highway.

Whatever the reason, by summer's end the whole project had been abandoned. From then until the summer of 1965, a hike to Cody became a must for our cabin guests. We were both fascinated and shocked that no attempt was ever made to salvage any of the lumber or equipment. Year after year we watched the deterioration of those expensive refrigerators and freezers, the collapse of the covered wagons, the disintegration of the upright piano, and the sagging of the walls of the fort.

But I'm getting ahead of my story. In the summer of 1957 we received a letter from Ward Newman informing us that our cabin was on his father's land. We contacted a lawyer, Sterling Gilbert. Through him we learned that the old town site of Gilpin had never been recorded. Much of it had been purchased by Dr. Newman. It and the Tregay property were now recorded and incorporated as Skydale, Inc.

We were advised by Mr. Gilbert that although we had only a quit-claim deed to our cabin and land, the fact that the property had been fenced in for over twenty years should allow us ownership by right of adverse possession. We decided to sit tight.

In December of that year, we received another letter, this time from Dr. J.M. himself. It stated that the area was being further developed by Skydale, Inc., that the surveyor was now pushing through the streets, and that property had doubled in value. " I am therefore requesting that you either move your cabin onto your own lot or purchase the lot on which it projects at a price of $500 within the next ten days." With some fear and foreboding we held our ground. (No pun intended.) That was the last we heard from the Newmans.

In the late 1950's or early '60's a contractor named Earl Hoffman bought the Newman property and began to develop our area into Skydale Acres Subdivision. He was able to get the financial backing to carry out his plan. The fort was bulldozed, and the old Tregay homestead was burned. That was a sad day for us. A hunk of history destroyed without any attempt at preservation. We managed to salvage some lumber from the fort and asked Hoffman if we might have the front door from the Tregay house. We took the middle panels out of the door and made a kitchen screen door for the cabin. Years later we found the seat from one of the covered wagons and placed it on a stump in the side yard of the cabin, a treasured reminder of times past.

As Skydale Acres was being developed, the question came up again as to who owned the land our cabin was sitting on. It was then discovered that a strip of government land, an old mining claim, cut across our side yard and took in the land under part of our kitchen, dining room, and living room. The rest of our fenced in yard now belonged to Hoffman. Fortunately, he was willing to sell us the part that did not belong to the government, and because of the configuration of the Skydale lots, the aspen grove west of the cabin, down to the road by Jim's spring, was included in our deed. A 1962 receipt from Hoffman shows that the total cost was $317.50, and I paid it off at $ 20 a month.

As old buildings were torn down and new houses were built, the area became well populated, and the old town site of Gilpin gave up all but a few of its ghosts. The only original structures remaining are the old boarding house, Merrill Slater's place up the hill north of us, and our own log cabin, which came to be known as The Ol' Timer. The Ol' Timer is the only original building which has not had any structural change. It is pictured and described in a book, *Ghost Towns of Colorado*.

Did I hear you ask where The Ol' Timer is located? Why, its in the ghost town of Gilpin, up Lump Gulch, across the road from the old boarding house.

As I am putting the finishing touches on these stories during the spring of 2002, I am thinking of Lump Gulch as it is today. According to Bonnie Cashion, our neighbor and historian, the count is now 96 family dwellings. The school bus drives past The Ol' Timer twice a day, collecting and distributing numbers of children. Large two-story homes, some with four or five bedrooms and as many baths, march up new roads toward Lindeman Peak and the top of Gamble Gulch. We watch folks move in and folks move out. Things change, but there are a few constants. I still own The Ol' Timer, and the government still owns a hunk of my land.

GIVING UP THE GHOST

*Fort Cody as it was tumbling down.
Photo around 1958.*

*Looking east from Ol' Timer to Jim Murray's cabin,
barn, shed, and the tip of his outhouse. The small
gray building (right) was a Gilpin original. It was
moved in the early '60's. Photo around 1955.*

*Two of the cabins from the old town of Gilpin. Torn down
sometime after 1971. The Hamilton cabin and The Ol' Timer in
the background.*

*The old boarding house from the mining days,
on Lump Gulch road in the town site of
Gilpin. It has been renovated and is now a
year-round residence.*

*Two of the cabins from the old town of Gilpin.
Torn down sometime after 1971.*

29

PROSPECTOR JIM

Mary O'Neill has written a book, *People I'd Like to Keep*, describing colorful people who have enriched her life. My old prospector friend, Jim Murray, was such a friend to me. When I think or speak or write about him, I know with certainty that he is one of my "forever friends."

Jim lived in the cabin next door to The Ol' Timer when we bought it in 1953. Our two dwellings were situated in what was then referred to as the ghost town of Gilpin, up Lump Gulch. Jim was eighty years old at the time, a little hard of hearing, and his eyesight wasn't as sharp as it had been. Although he was quite content with his own company, he was always excited when we Kansans arrived for the summer. Our guests were his guests, and he showed them through his three-room cabin with great pride.

He loved to tell stories of early days, especially when he and his wife Annie had lived in Gilpin during the gold rush days.

Prospector Jim in front of the home he built in early 1940's.

When the mines were shut down in the early 1900's, he and Annie had moved to Denver where he got a job working with a wrecking crew. When Annie died in the early forties, Jim again felt the call of his old haunts. As soon as he was old enough to draw his old age pension, he moved back to Gilpin. He had saved lumber from buildings he had wrecked, and he used it to build his house, a garage, a shed, and an outhouse. He couldn't have been more proud of his accomplishments. Winter and summer he cooked and heated with wood and coal stoves, penetrated the darkness with kerosene lamps, and hauled water from a spring a half block

Jim and wife Annie on the porch of their Gilpin home in early 1900's.

west of his cabin. He kept the spring boarded and cleaned, and after we became neighbors, he shared it with us. Never was there more delicious, clear, cold water than that which we hauled in a galvanized bucket from the spring, through our aspen grove, and onto our kitchen counter.

Jim liked for his guests to know that music was an important part of his life. He had a wind-up phonograph in his living room, and above it hung his guitar. Though the guitar lacked strings and the wind-up was missing the crank, the display of these items gave Jim a chance to mention his musical accomplishments. He had done a lot of singing and playing at dances and parties in his day, including many neighborhood gatherings at The Ol' Timer, then called Snowcrest. He had even written several songs and still had a copy of one which had been published.

Friend Jim was a bearer of gifts. We could never get ahead of him. If we took him a new oilcloth covering for his kitchen table, he was soon at our door with candy bars. In exchange for homemade cookies, he might offer a colorful rock or a rare piece of wood he'd found on one of his walks. One of his gifts was a piece of driftwood that resembled a duck in flight. He was delighted that we could envision it, too.

One of Jim's favorite songs was "There's a Long, Long Trail A-Winding." We had a recording of it in the cupboard of our own wind-up phonograph, and Jim used to come over just to hear it. He'd push the wicker rocker close to the speaker so he could hear, and as he listened he'd rock and whistle softly. His eyes were a beautiful transparent blue, and in his expression was a deep peace. It was a calming experience just to sit with him.

Jim had not returned to the mountains to retire. He staked a claim on a slope leading to Lindeman Peak, about a mile and a half south of his cabin, and he continued to prospect with regularity. We were both amused and concerned as we'd see him trudge off to his claim, The Olive Lode, with his sack of dynamite, his pick, and his shovel. He never seemed discouraged over his lack of success. With great enthusiasm he'd sing the praises of this activity. He'd stop at The Ol' Timer on his return from a day of mining and exclaim, "It's the most exciting work there is. You never know when the next blast will bring a million." Then he'd promise that when he struck it rich I'd never have to teach again. I didn't hold my breath or consider giving up my job, but I valued the promise and the sincerity with which it was given.

From late August when we shuttered the windows and headed home until early June when we returned to our mountains, he kept a constant check on cabin and grounds, nailing a loose shutter here, replacing a roof shingle there. We corresponded throughout the months of separation, and I regret that I did not keep his letters. They would be a reminder of the joy and contentment of simple living.

We had been home just a month in the fall of 1959 when we received a letter and newspaper clipping from his sister-in-law, Vera Neal, who lived in Moon Gulch, two gulches to the north. It read:

Little Hope Prospector Will Be Found Alive

Denver Post Special
GILPIN, Colo., Sept. 26—

Virtually all hope was abandoned Saturday that James Murray, 87, would be found alive.

More than 70 searchers, in jeeps and on horseback, set out at dawn Saturday to look for the old-age pensioner and part-time prospector with a warning from Sheriff Tom Collins that Murray may have been killed for his money.

Murray's sister-in-law, Mrs. Vera Neal, who discovered him missing from his three-room cabin here about 4:30 p. m. Wednesday, told the Gilpin County Sheriff Murray generally carried his life savings—about $300—on his person.

Collins said he certainly could not rule out the possibility of foul play. But he admitted he had no definite leads.

"But I don't see how Murray can still be alive," he said.

The Sheriff said search parties would try to cover a three-mile radius from the cabin Saturday.

Murray, who suffered from high blood pressure and an enlarged heart, apparently was on a search for firewood when he left his cabin. A check of his wardrobe by Mrs. Neal indicated he was wearing only a pair of work trousers, shirt, light wool sweater, shoes and a cap.

Murray had lived alone, in the cabin he built himself, for the past 17 years.

Until the past year he had worked his mining claim, "The Olive Lode," located 1 1/2 miles south of his cabin.

He often jokingly told Mrs. Neal the silver and gold in The Olive Lode "would put Gilpin County on the map one of these days."

Mrs. Neal said he still liked to tramp the woods alone. She said he had recently requested that "There's a Gold Mine in the Sky" be sung at his funeral.

It was hard enough to lose Jim, but what haunted his loved ones during that cold, miserable winter was the uncertainty of the circumstances surrounding his death. Wonderings and imaginings of the suffering he might have endured couldn't be put to rest until his remains were found and given an appropriate burial.

On June 3 the following spring, Mr. and Mrs. Charles Lerch returned from their winter home in Denver to their summer cabin at the Smuggler Mine in Travis Gulch, a branch of neighboring Gamble Gulch. The Lerches were enjoying a mountain walk up the hill from their cabin when they saw a shiny object hanging from a tree limb. The rest of the story is told in the following newspaper account:

Central City, Colorado — Friday, June 3, 1960

Body of Jim Murray, Missing for 8 Months, Found Two Miles from His Gilpin Home

The body of 87 year old Jim Murray, missing since last September 3rd, was found near Perigo last Friday by Mr. and Mrs. Charles Lerch, who had arrived to open their cabin and then took a walk in the area.

Murray apparently died either of a heart attack or exposure, not the victim of foul play as had been feared. A "Swede Saw" belonging to Murray was found hanging on a tree near the body, and money he carried when he left the cabin was still in two wallets on his body.

The elderly man had left his cabin in Gilpin, in the central part of the county, sometime during the morning of Wednesday, September 23, with the fire still burning in the wood stove. He was in his slippers and had left his false teeth and hearing aid at the house.

The absence was discovered by Mr. and Mrs. Mike Neal who had an appointment to meet him that afternoon. The cabin was empty when they arrived at 4:30, and they waited until six o'clock. When Murray did not return, they called Sheriff Tom Collins.

A search was started immediately, and went on into early Thursday morning. More than a hundred persons were in the area on Thursday for the search, which continued through the start of a mixture of rain and snow. Searching continued, and more volunteers arrived for the weekend.

The light snow and below freezing nighttime temperatures continued over the weekend, and heavy snow Monday night stalled everything. However, searching has been going on sporadically through the winter, with some of Murray's many friends from the Rollinsville and Nederland areas going into the high country on snowshoes to check out various areas.

Sheriff Collins said Murray's body was partially under a tree, where he might have crawled to get out of the weather. He said the body was torn by animals, and there was no definite way to establish the cause of death.

Collins said the body was found about two miles from his cabin, in a densely wooded area about 25 feet from the top of a mountain. Access to the area was by Gamble Gulch, Collins said.

Gilpin, where Murray lived, is twelve miles north of Black Hawk and about two miles from highway 119.

Jim's body was cremated and his ashes buried in the front yard of his home. The cabin had several different owners before sister Marj and brother-in-law Robert were able to purchase it. A couple of interesting things have happened to convince us that Jim is still visiting our two summer homes, still looking out for us. One winter some friends of our neighbors, Bonnie and George Merchant, offered to care-take The Ol' Timer in exchange for the use of it on special occasions. They knew nothing of Jim or our stories about him. Therefore, we were quite surprised when we learned that while they were cleaning the living room in preparation for a Thanksgiving gathering, the old rocker sitting in the corner began to rock. Though no one was near it, it just kept rocking, and as they watched, they felt a calming presence. They told Bonnie, and Bonnie told us, and from the description we knew it was the old wicker rocker, Jim's favorite chair, the one he sat in by the phonograph when he was listening to the song he loved, "There's A Long, Long, Trail A-Winding."

After Hamiltons purchased Jim's cabin, they rented it one winter to a young man who was a friend of our next-door neighbors, the Haberkorns. One night this fellow, whose name I can't remember, swore he heard all kinds of tramping and carrying on in the attic. He tore out of Jim's house and over to Haberkorns, waking them with the story that there was a ghost in his house. He was sure the place was haunted. We were pleased.

I am also pleased that Jim is at home in his own front yard, now known as the Hamilton's front yard. There is a mound of rocks over the spot where Jim's ashes are buried, and as I traipse back and forth between our two cabins I sometimes stop for a chat with my "forever friend."

One day after I had been telling some visitors about Jim, I started jotting a poem about him, and the poem became a song, a ballad to Prospector Jim. Want to sing along?

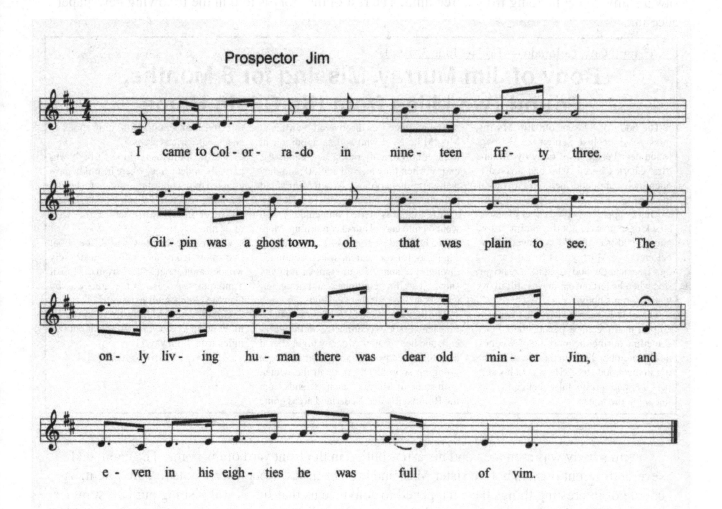

Prospector Jim

I came to Col-or-ra-do in nine-teen fif-ty three.

Gil-pin was a ghost town, oh that was plain to see. The

on-ly liv-ing hu-man there was dear old min-er Jim, and

e-ven in his eigh-ties he was full of vim.

PROSPECTOR JIM

I came to Colorado in 1953.
Gilpin was a ghost town, oh, that was plain to see.
The only living human there was dear old miner Jim,
And even in his 80's he was full of vim.

The first thing when he'd meet you he'd show you through his place.
It wasn't any palace and it didn't have much space.
But it was put together by the work of his own hand.
To him it was the greatest place in all this mighty land.

Now old Jim kept on mining after it was out of style.
He said there'd come a day when he would bring home quite a pile.
And with that million dollar blast, he didn't know just when,
He'd set me up on Easy Street, I'd never teach again.

Jim Murray never struck it rich and I am teaching still.
But summer days the ghost of him goes striding up the hill.
His dynamite is in his pack, his pick is by his side.
His sky blue eyes look straight ahead, he holds himself with pride.

The memories of that dear old friend more precious are than gold.
I hope that I will have his zest as I am growing old.
When it was time, he sat right down beneath a tree to die,
And said, "Dear God, I'm ready for my gold mine in the sky."

IN DEFENSE OF OUTHOUSES

WRITTEN IN 1984

Tonight as I took my bedtime trip to the cabin outhouse, I left the door ajar and watched the moon as it lit up the yard, silhouetting the cabin and the Colorado Spruce by my kitchen door. I thought of the many evenings and nights I have sat in my home in the city unaware of the moon's waxings and wanings, of full moons with their enchantments. It reminded me that my trips to the outhouse have often put me in touch with sights and sounds of nature that I would otherwise have missed. I thought of this chapter I've been planning to write for my book and felt inspired to begin.

I first knew that I had to write "In Defense of Outhouses," when my niece Sally came home from a conference and mentioned that the speaker had made derogatory remarks about outhouses. "How dare anyone speak disparagingly of outhouses," I objected. "Some of my most pleasant memories are associated with that ancient necessity." "How so?" asked Sally. "Glad you asked," I responded enthusiastically, and I began to reminisce.

The "house out back" was kind of a playhouse for Ted and me in the early years before first grade came along and took away my freedom. Ted Baehni was the neighbor boy when my family lived on "The Ranch" at the edge of town in Holton, Kansas. He was a year my junior, the only neighbor near my age, and we were constant companions. When one of us had to interrupt our game of make-believe for that necessary trip to the outhouse, the other went along for company. While there, we would browse through the "Monkey Ward" catalogue, planning our futures, picking out what we would look like, what we would wear, our furniture, etc.

I haven't seen Ted in years, but I've kept up with his career and his whereabouts. Last fall when I was in the town where he lives, I called and left a message on his answering machine. "Hey, Ted," I said, "if you don't have anything better to do when you get home, call your old outhouse buddy at 325-3226. And he did. We talked and laughed about old times and the fun we'd had planning our lives in the old outhouse in the days of innocence before we knew that boys were boys and girls were girls, and you weren't supposed to share such intimacies.

Although the Ranch privy itself was not a thing of beauty, Mom's flower garden surrounding it was. She had hollyhocks growing in front and to the sides of the steps. They grew tall and had blossoms in varying shades, from soft pink to deep wine. After completing my outhouse visits, I would often stop to pick a bud and a fully opened flower to fashion into a doll. The bud was the head and the full flower was the flaring skirt. To this day I associate hollyhocks with outhouses and vice-versa. It's a pleasant association.

In 1935, when I was nine years old, our family moved from my birthplace. Our new home had indoor plumbing, but I was able to continue my friendship with outhouses whenever I visited my oldest sister and her family on their farm each summer. Now it became a hideout, a place to slip off to when I wanted to read, or when dishes were to be done. I often left the door ajar so that I could watch the farm animals, especially the chickens and the farm cats. One of the paths from the outhouse led to the back yard and the orchard where apples, plums, or pears might be ripe for the picking.

Sometime during my high school years the farmhouse was modernized and there were no more outhouses in my life, at least none with such pleasant memories. There would be one occasionally at a park or picnic area, but you know about those. They can't be included in my "Defense of Outhouses" for obvious reasons.

In 1953, when the Kivetts and I bought Snowcrest, now called The Ol' Timer, my love affair with outhouses was rekindled. Like the cabin, the accompanying outhouse is very old, but it has continued to serve a great many people each summer since we took possession. Various guests have contributed to its upkeep. It has had new supports, new stoop, several new hand rails, and numerous contributions have been made to its interior decorating. Poems have included such relics as, "Mary had a little watch. She swallowed it one day. And now she takes her castor oil to pass the time away." Friends and relatives have added such corny captions as "The job is never finished 'til the paper work is done," and "We aim to please. You aim too, please." At one time the Gilpin Annex, as it is called, was a community showplace. People in neighboring gulches would ask to come see it. In those days hill folks were hard up for entertainment.

My niece Jan is almost as fond of outhouses as I am. She leaves the door open, day or night, and might be seen reading, feeding chipmunks, or playing "throw the stick" with the neighbor dog. Since it is a three-holer, she likes to accompany others to the throne and share secrets with them.

Niece Sally has not been so fond of the little room out back since the time she dropped her husband Alan's car keys down the hole. She came out the door hollering, "Get me a flashlight and a hanger!" but wouldn't tell what had happened.

We've had some good family fun over the Gilpin Annex. One year my brother Bob and his family came to visit from Washington state. Bob's son Larry was into electronics and working with sound effects for school plays. He brought a microphone, speaker, and whatever equipment he needed for wiring a sound system to the outhouse. He hid a small speaker under one of the seats and attached it to a microphone which he concealed in the back room of the cabin. When brother Glen went up the path, Larry said into the mike, "Would you please move over? I'm working down here." We expected Glen to come flying out in a fluster. Instead, he walked calmly back to the cabin and didn't say a word about the experience. When we realized he wasn't going to offer any comment, we questioned his reaction to the incident. Glen replied in a stoic manner, "I just said to the guy down there, 'You tend to your business and I'll tend to mine.'"

Glen and family gave me a great Christmas gift in 1955, after their first summer visit to the cabin. It was a beautifully preserved cow skull they'd found while walking on the Indian Reservation near Mayetta, Kansas. Glen wrote a poem about it which is a family masterpiece. We named the skull Elsie, and each summer it hangs at the outhouse entrance. The poem and picture of Glen presenting it to me hang inside for all to read and enjoy.

ODE TO ELSIE

by Glen F. Rings

Many things both odd and pretty
Festoon homes in Gilpin City,
Gifts from kinfolk, gifts from friends,
Things retrieved, odds and ends.

In the cabin called Ol' Timer,
Covered o'er with vines and climber,
Dwell the Kansas Educators
When Kansas sun will fry pertaters.

Ol' Timer's furnishings are many,
Some cost some, and some not any.
For instance, there's Old Drum,
Former contents worse than Rum.
Now it stands an invitation
For any generous donation.

And a bucket used for ore
Reminds us of our mining lore.
Ore was its intended load,
It just stood there by the road.

Many relatives and friends
Spend vacations and weekends
Ol' Timer's guests, a jovial group,
Eating all from nuts to soup.

For these hostesses so kind
Some fitting gift we had to find.
Aught of value all seemed dross,
Causing us financial loss.

Then one day when nature beckoned,
Traveling where no one had reckoned,
Came this object into view,
And at once we thought of you.

How Ol' Timer's rustic look,
Western as a Zane Grey book,
Could be enhanced by such a find

O'er the front door or behind.
Now old Elsie, noble creature,
Evidenced by every feature,
Left this life, and left in leaving
Much besides a sense of grieving,
Left this skull of bone so white,
It will glisten in the night
Welcoming traveler, informing guest,
"This is it! You've reached the West."

Brother Glen: "Merry Christmas, Esther. We found Elsie as we were enjoying a Sunday stroll."

Esther: "Great! Perfect! I have just the spot for it."

39

There are many other privy tales, such as the midnight adventure of our friend Galen Ewing. He was strolling up the path in the deep, dark of night when he heard the sound of wild animals in the woods behind the outhouse. He went tearing back to the cabin to find that the door had locked behind him. Instead of waking anyone, he spent the rest of the night in his Nash Rambler.

Some of the younger generation who didn't grow up with outhouses are appalled at the idea. Others can't figure out how it works. Great-niece Margie first came to the cabin when she was very small. After her first trip up the hill she came running into the house asking, "Grandma, where do you flush?"

"You don't," said Grandma Marj. "But Grandma," replied Margie, "Momma says you're supposed to flush at everybody's house."

For the most part, outhouses are a thing of the past, and for good reason. I know that I should get rid of my Gilpin Annex. One day the health department will say I must. Until then, I'll keep it and the nostalgia that goes with it. I'll continue to enjoy the things I hear and see as nature's insistent call propels me from the cabin into the fresh and exciting out-of-doors. And who knows, maybe next year I'll plant hollyhocks in front of the stoop.

YEAR 2002

As Lump Gulch continued to grow from the ghost town of 1953 to a subdivision of ninety plus family dwellings, the County Health Department did indeed make rulings that encouraged us to get on with plans for an indoor facility. The millennium year seemed the appropriate time, and on a June day, 2000, we celebrated our first flush. The outhouse still stands, though leaning a little more each year, an historic landmark with its weathered wood and corrugated tin roof. Elsie the cow skull still glistens as the moonlight washes over the back yard, and on clear summer nights the big dipper takes its place directly over the outhouse. We keep the path clear, and once in a while I get the urge to "run up the hill" to the Gilpin Annex.

As a postscript to the defense of outhouses, I should probably mention that there were downsides to these nostalgic strolls to connect with nature. One was the yearly dig. Each spring when we first arrived, I donned my J.C. Penney work boots and my fashion plate muck-green jumpsuit, and with shovel, sack, and the help of loyal family members, shoveled the past year's outhouse build-up. Just when this heavy work was beginning to take a toll on my aging back, I discovered a fine, strong young man who would do the job for $15. That was money cheerfully spent.

Another job, not so hard on the back but also unpleasant, was the morning trip to empty the chamber pot. My outhouse outfit was greatly admired by our many guests. The lovely pink robe was at least 25 years old when it was seized, stolen, and replaced by some Kansas admirers. The boots were men's suede, a size or two too large, but worked well with heavy duty red wool socks. They were waterproof, probably due to the accumulation of dirt and grime collected over the years.

IN DEFENSE OF OUTHOUSES

Niece Jan and her grandson Jonathan Pearson. Jan leaves the outhouse door open day or night. She doesn't want to miss anything.

The morning chamber pot chore has never been a favorite, but at least I have the proper attire.

Even dog Whitey was drawn to the outhouse.

Each spring I don my J.C. Penney work boots and my fashion statement muck-green jump suit, grab my shovel, and go to work. This year, Marj and Jan helped.

JEEPERS! WHAT'S A FOUR-WHEEL DRIVE?

It must have been the summer of 1963 when Betty Campbell and I hauled our first four-wheel drive to Colorado. We had decided we needed a rugged vehicle for exploring our mountains. It wasn't that our regular cars hadn't taken us to plenty of out-of-the-way places. Whitie, the 1960 Buick with its four-barrel carburetor, would walk straight up the side of a mountain, but usually at considerable cost and inconvenience. Its low-slung bottom suffered from leaky oil pans, bent fly-wheels, jammed emergency brake, damaged tires, and scratched paint. And it wasn't that we were too lazy to walk. When we got as far as vehicles would take us, we'd hoof it to high mountain lakes and breathtaking vistas. But there were still trails that demanded a four-wheel drive, and we were determined to see it all.

Sometime during the previous winter we had asked Betty's brother Howard, who lived in Kansas City, to be on the lookout for an older model jeep that, in his judgment, would be pretty reliable. We thought we could manage as much as $150 for such a purchase. We were ecstatic when he called to say that he'd found just the thing. It was a 1948 Willys station wagon with red and white paint, what was left of it. The next weekend we hurried to Kansas City, drove it around a block or two and claimed it for our own, referring to it as "our Willy."

We were both teaching at Kansas State Teacher's College in Emporia, Kansas, that summer, so Willy sat in Howard's yard till the first of August when we were ready to travel west. It was a scorching hot day when we loaded the Buick, hooked Willy on behind with a U-Haul trailer hitch, and left Kansas City. The U-Haul attendant gave us a warning which we intended to heed. "Don't, under any circumstance, try to back up with this trailer hitch."

Progress was slow, and we were barely into Western Kansas when it was time to eat our picnic lunch. We started looking for a roadside park with an entrance and an exit, and found what we thought was a drive-through picnic area. What we didn't know until it was too late was that there was a row of posts dividing the two sides of the park. Once we were in, there was no way out but to back up. We had visions of tearing the hitch to pieces and having to use rope and baling wire the rest of the trip. But by inching backwards ever so carefully, we somehow managed to get turned around and back onto the highway. By four P.M. we were only as far as Hays, Kansas. The car was running a little hot, and so were we, so we decided to stop for the night and start again before daylight the next morning. When we tried making turns into and around the town, looking for a motel, we discovered that there was a problem with Willy's steering. Whenever we made a turn, Willy went straigh, and could only skid around corners. To solve the problem, it was necessary to take turns riding in Willy so we could steer him. We twisted and turned our way to a motel where we slept till three A.M. Since we were starting off again in the dark, we needed a taillight on the jeep, but when we tried the lights, they wouldn't work. This was serious. It called for creativity. The best we could do was take the flashlight from the car and tie it to Willy's back bumper. Fortunately there were no cops around that time of morning.

It was mid-afternoon on Sunday when we made our way, one of us in each car, through downtown Denver to the U-Haul place on Federal Boulevard. We separated the two vehicles and returned the U-Haul trailer hitch. "Okay Willy," I said with confidence, "you're on your own." You'd think we might have suspected a dead battery when the lights didn't work, but we were taken by surprise when we turned the key in the jeep and nothing happened. Even on Sunday Federal Boulevard is a busy street, but we were so anxious to complete our trip that instead of having the battery charged, we got the U-Haul attendants to push us down the thoroughfare to a start. I was in the lead in Willy and Betty was behind in the Buick. For some reason, I can't imagine why, we decided on the Wondervu route to the cabin. This is a winding, drop-off kind of road that is frightening in the best of vehicles. It began to rain and I turned on the wipers. They worked fine on the level road, but when we began to climb and I had to floor-board the accelerator, the wipers went dead. There was enough juice for one or the other, but not for both. We solved this by putting Betty in the lead, and I followed her taillight as we crept around one precarious curve after another. Our arrival at the cabin was spectacular. Sisters Marj and June were there with their spouses, Robert and Chic. Brother Glen and wife Nell had arrived. Friends Doris and Charles Sheetz, Edna and Rex Scott, and Galen and Ula Ewing had joined the party, and I can't even remember how many offspring of these couples completed the group that filed out to greet us. The men were immediately taken with the jeep and began a thorough inspection.

"How do you put it into four-wheel drive?" asked Robert who always wants to understand everything.

"I don't know," I replied. "Isn't it always in four-wheel drive?"

"Just a minute," said Galen, the mechanical wizard. "This jeep doesn't have four-wheel drive." We looked on in disbelief as he explained. "There are no hubs, no levers, no special gears, no sign indicating this special feature. This is not a four-wheel drive vehicle."

"Oh, well," we concluded, "it will still take us places we wouldn't want to take a car." It was high-centered so it wouldn't scrape the rocks, and it certainly wouldn't matter if it got scratched.

Enthusiasm dies hard in our family, especially at get-togethers, so as soon as we had eaten and visited awhile, we were ready to give family and guests a ride. I have a better understanding, as I look back on the event, why it was that only the women and children piled into Willy for a thrilling ride over the worst road we could think of, the Gap Road. The Gap is between Mt. Thorodin and Bear Mountain off highway 119 east of the cabin. It eventually comes out on Highway 72 and back through Wondervu, from whence Betty and I had just come. The Gap isn't a bad road now, but in those early days it was pretty awful. What made it worth doing was the spectacular scenery. Our congenial passengers were full of enthusiasm and appreciation, and we returned home at dusk praising all things, especially Willy. The next morning, however, Willy wouldn't start. No amount of pushing would convince it to turn over. We called the Rollinsville mechanic, Francis Cielehof, who came and towed our purchase off to his house for an appraisal. His report was not good. "This is a pretty sick buggy," said Francis. "It would take quite a bit of work and money to put this jeep into any kind of condition for driving these mountains." We didn't have any more money to invest in it, so we asked if he could sell it for junk. Before we left to go back to Kansas, we went to say goodbye to our Willy, and our dream of high mountain jeeping. I noticed something under the driver's seat and pulled out what appeared to be a riding stick. It had a jade looking fox-head handle with a ruby eye. The handle slipped out of a leather casing and exposed a sharp pointed sword. We felt certain it must be a valuable antique. We took it home and gave it a place of honor on the dining room wall. We've never had it appraised, but we like to think that it's worth what we lost on our venture. The next winter, Francis sold Willy for $75. It was 1969 before we got an honest-to-goodness four-wheel drive. But—that's another story.

BAD BUY AND TOHO

If you have read the chapter just before this one, you know that our first jeep was not a four-wheel drive. The next time we went looking for a mountain vehicle, we saw to it that it had locking hubs, a special lever for engaging the four-wheel drive, and the words "four-wheel drive" on the body. As before, the choice had to fit the pocketbook, and this time, the summer of 1969, we had saved $800. We visited a number of used car dealerships in Boulder and settled on a 1954 Willys army jeep. It had a black body and an off-white canvas top with isinglass windows. There was fairly comfortable seating for the driver and one passenger. A couple of metal side benches over the back tires allowed uncomfortable seating for two to four more passengers, depending on their size and endurance.

We never stuck to one name for this vehicle. Sometimes we called it "Jeeper," and sometimes "Blacky," and when it was costing a hunk for repairs, which was pretty often, we referred to it as "Bad Buy."

"Bad Buy" was unique in a number of ways, but two of them were especially troublesome. The first was the door on the driver's side. We'd be sailing through the streets of Boulder or up the canyon toward Rollinsville when suddenly the door would fly open and start flapping in the breeze. It was a gymnastic feat to reach out far enough to catch the door with my left hand and still keep my eyes on the road. The right hand was plenty busy steering and shifting. In winter it could be an invigorating ride.

Second were the windshield wipers. The left one was battery powered, but the right one had to be operated by hand. If you didn't have a co-pilot in the seat next to you to flip the wipers back and forth, your right hand took on an extra chore. It had to steer, shift, and clean the windshield while your left hand was busy with the door.

During the winter of 1970, fellow teacher Betty Campbell and I took a leave of absence from our Kansas teaching jobs and went to school in Boulder. We drove "Jeeper" the twenty-four miles up Boulder Canyon to the cabin every weekend. We gained new respect for it as it plowed through three feet of snow and started, though reluctantly, in sub-zero weather. It had no heater, was using oil, and seemed to be losing power on the steep grades, but it never failed to get us where we wanted to go.

By summer we had to do something about our second "bad buy." We needed a better four-wheel drive. As luck would have it, one of our cabin visitors from Kansas City took a liking to "Blackie" and purchased it for $200. He towed it home, put a blade on the front of it, and used it to clear snow from parking lots in the winter. He named it "Good Buy," and it made him a lot of money. Our business transaction, buying for $800 and selling for $200, was in keeping with the financial modeling I got from sister Marj. She always laughed about how she seemed to buy things for more than they were worth and sell them for less than their value. "Buy high and sell low" was our motto.

Again Betty and I went in search of an upgrade. This time we were ready to invest $1500. That amount bought us a 1967 Toyota Land Cruiser station wagon. It was a beauty with red bottom and white top, and hardly a scratch or dent. The odometer read 1500 miles. We were later to question its accuracy, but it was still a good deal. This vehicle was big, with cushioned bench seats front and back, wide enough to hold three people each. We could crowd two more guests and picnic supplies into the back end through the tailgate. If two of the passengers were children, we could squeeze in nine passengers plus the driver. We only did this for short distances, on the back roads to our favorite picnic spots.

I had been working part-time at a pre-school in Boulder and had just read the children a story about Toho the Terribly Terrific Tiger. That gave us an idea for naming our new purchase. We christened it Toho the Terribly Terrific Toyota. Toho for short. It lent itself to , "Whoa, Toho," "Oh, no, Toho," "Let's go, Toho," "Good show, Toho," and on and on.

As I write this story, I'm thinking about the love affair I've had with Toho, and of our many thrills, adventures, frustrations, and narrow escapes. There was the time the wiring got screwed up, and every time we'd turn a corner, the horn would honk. And there was the summer we couldn't shift into reverse and had to plan all of our trips with room for turn-around. One year the tailgate didn't want to stay shut, and on one of our trips up Rollins Pass, the accelerator got stuck. Each winter when I returned to Kansas or Arizona to my teaching job, I'd leave Toho in Colorado with friends and strangers, with mechanics and cabin caretakers. Most springs he needed minor surgery to get him in shape for the impossible trails he'd be asked to maneuver. In the spring of 1984, after having left him with the friend of a friend, I hastened to his winter storage place to find him in a very sad condition. He had no brakes, no clutch, no battery. His paint was curling on top, and the inside was thick with dirt and grease. I told myself the time had come to put him to sleep. He was beyond repair. He had done his job faithfully and well, and I should let him rest in peace. I would call the wrecker service and have him hauled to the junkyard. But on my way to the cabin phone, I got to thinking. What would summers in Colorado be without the excitement of those high country, four-wheel drive adventures? By the time I reached the telephone I'd come to my senses. I called a wrecker service and told the driver to haul Toho to the Toyota garage in Boulder. I instructed the mechanics to do whatever it would take to bring my trusty steed back to life.

The repair bill was only $400, but it seemed a lot, considering I had been on leave without pay for a year. However, the trip home from Boulder after his "fixing" was worth the price. We roared up the old Magnolia Road, snaking around curve after curve. I sang and shouted to the sky, the wind, and the mountains. We literally danced our way back to the cabin. I said to myself, "How many times in your life can you buy ecstasy for $400?"

Toho still needed a paint job, but I was so pleased and proud to have him up and running that I planned a jeep trip for the next day. Marj, Robert and I went tearing up the road above Rollinsville to Gooches to pick up our friend Florence, who was as ready for adventure as I was. I puffed up with pride as I showed her my rejuvenated buggy. She got in and shut the door. It bounced open. She shut it again, and again it swung open. "Hmm, that must be something they forgot to fix," I reasoned. Well, we couldn't let a broken door stop us. We got a piece of rope and tied it across to a handle on the dash. Parts for a 1967 Toyota are scarce and expensive. I'd just wait till next summer to deal with it. For the ten weeks we drove Toho that summer, the front seat passengers slid through from the driver's side. A broken door didn't stop us from having another wonderful season with Toho, The Terribly Terrific Toyota.

The following summer, 1985, I decided to paint Toho myself. I scraped the peeling paint off as best I could, sanded down the rough spots, and using rust-proof paint and brush, gave my buggy a refresher coat. It looked pretty good for a few years, but by 1998, it definitely needed a professional job. The Earl Scheib special, which was advertised at $400, actually cost $1000, and it took three tense trips to Denver to get the job done decently, with Toho shaking and swaying down the freeway at an unprecedented speed of 60 mph. However, I was repaid by the admiring looks Toho and I received. As I was returning from Denver with my newly painted pride and joy, I chose again to take the Magnolia Road from Boulder to highway 119 above Nederland. As I came to one of the few straight stretches on that hairpin, steep-hill road, a car slowed in passing, and a woman stuck her head out the passenger window. "That's a beauty of a buggy you got there!" she shouted.

Toho had many admirers. It was not unusual to return to his parking place to find two or three people, usually men, checking him out. They'd want to know what year he was, how long I'd had him, how he performed, etc. Steve, my faithful mechanic in Nederland, took pride in keeping Toho running. When I paid him for repair work, his receipts would have such comments as, "The greatest four-wheel drive ever made." There were those who had the nerve to ask if I'd sell him. One young man in particular, Kena Twigg-Smith, a resident of Nederland, seven miles down the road from the cabin, had his heart set on owning my Toyota. I was working around the cabin one day in 1999 when the phone rang. I answered with my usual, "This is the Ol' Timer up Lump Gulch."

"Yeah," came the voice from the other end of the line, "I'm Kena, the guy who's been wanting to buy your Toyota. Any chance you'd sell it this summer?"

"Not a chance."

"Not for any price?"

"Well, what did you have in mind?"

"Oh, I was thinking maybe four or five thousand."

"Not interested."

"I could probably go as high as seven thousand."

Thinking he'd reached his ceiling, I said, "I'd have to have at least eight."

A short pause, and then, "Yeah? Well, I could probably get hold of that much."

"Well, I'm not sure, I'd have to think it over." I hung up and sat staring into space.

There was plenty to think about. Toho had cost me $1500 in repairs that summer and had still refused to start a couple of times. I was going to be spending a lot of money on a new indoor bathroom during the following winter and was dipping into my retirement savings to do it. I could surely use the money. When would I ever again get such an offer? Without consulting anyone about my decision, I called Kena within the hour. "It's a deal," I said, and two days later we made our exchange.

There will never be another Toho. Last summer, 2001, Sally bought a new 4-Runner, a beautiful Toyota we call Silver. The hubs engage with the flip of a lever. It has power steering and power brakes. There are no fumes, no rattles. You can carry on conversations while the motor's running. It has never honked of its own accord when we turn a corner or refused to shift. Everything works, including the heater. It takes us anywhere we want to go. But it's not Toho. The love affair with my red and white tank continues. Through memories, stories, and photos of our high mountain adventures, Toho will always be mine. Once in a while I find myself singing the song I wrote about Toho, The Terribly Terrific Toyota, king of the four-wheel drive.

Toho, The Terribly Terrific Toyota

chorus

Toho, the Ter-ri-bly Ter-ri-fic Toyota, King of the four-wheel drive

1,2,3,   to coda on 4th ending

verse Toho, the Terribly terrific Toyota how do you ever survive?

For its bounce rat-tle bump on the old back roads,

And its tilt, shift, grind, and groan with the loads.

And it's "To - ho go," and it's "To - ho Whoa!"

And its "To - ho, why do you go so slow?"

coda

We're keep - ing you a - live.

TOHO, THE TERRIBLY TERRIFIC TOYOTA

Chorus

Toho, the Terribly Terrific Toyota, king of the four-wheel drive,
Toho, the Terribly Terrific Toyota, how do you ever survive?

Verse

For it's bounce, rattle, bump on the old back roads,
And it's tilt, shift, grind and groan with the loads.
And it's "Toho, go," and it's "Toho, whoa!,"
And it's, "Toho, why do you go so slow?"

Chorus

Toho, the Terribly Terrific Toyota, king of the four-wheel drive,
Toho, the Terribly Terrific Toyota, how do you ever survive?

Verse

It's engage those hubs and put it in low,
Then it's shift to Granny and away we go,
And it's wade the streams and it's go to the dump,
And it's haul wood and water and bring home junk.

Chorus

Toho, the Terribly Terrific Toyota, king of the four-wheel drive,
Toho, the Terribly Terrific Toyota, how do you ever survive?

Verse

Oh the paint's all gone, and the mirror sags,
And the gears won't shift, and the tailgate drags,
And the door flies open, and the signal's gone,
But still Toho keeps a-chuggin' along.

Chorus

Toho, the Terribly Terrific Toyota, king of the four-wheel drive,
Toho, the Terribly Terrific Toyota, how do you ever survive?

Verse

For there's still Loch Lomond and James Peak, too,
And Corona Pass, and there's Caribou,
And Gamble Gulch where we say good-bye,
So, Toho, you see why you cannot die.

Chorus

Toho, the Terribly Terrific Toyota, king of the four-wheel drive,
Toho, the Terribly Terrific Toyota, *(Coda)* We're keeping you alive.

BAD BUY AND TOHO

We gained new respect for Bad Buy as it plowed through three feet of snow and started in sub-zero weather.

"Can we maneuver this dilapidated bridge?" I asked. Toho was fearless. I wasn't.

Why did my passengers always dismount when I got to this stretch of the road on the way to Henry's Park?

"Should we try it?" "What have we got to lose?" came the reply. The seven passengers, some in their eighties, got out and walked up the steep hill. I shifted into "granny" and Toho did the rest.

I was too busy painting my trusty steed to stop for lunch. Marj fed me.

$8,000? The keys are yours, Kena. But in my heart, Toho The Terribly Terrific Toyota will always be mine.

MYRT NERHEIM, A LUMP GULCH ORIGINAL

Myrtle Tregay Nerheim was the undisputed authority when it came to the history of northern Gilpin County, especially the Lump Gulch/Gamble Gulch territory. She was the only old timer we knew who had lived most of her life up Lump Gulch. It was my personal loss that I spent so many summers at the cabin before getting acquainted with this delightful wisp of a woman and her two married daughters, Helen Kindler and Betty Huntsman. I had always admired her neat log cabin with its green roof and well-tended yard. It reminded me of pictures of mountain cabins, the "spot that's known to God alone, just a place to call our own," kind of cabin. It was nestled in an open meadow at the edge of the woods with a great view of Thorodin, Lazy Squaw, and Bear Mountains. Because it was at the end of the Lump Gulch road and some distance up the hill from their gated driveway, we just never seemed to get around to hiking up and getting acquainted. Besides, we were always busy doing cabin projects or showing our Kansas friends our mountains.

In 1969-70, the year Betty Campbell and I stayed in Colorado to go to school at Colorado University in Boulder, we finally took time to go knocking on Myrt's door. We received such a warm welcome and had so much to share that the friendship was immediate. Each summer after that first meeting, the Nerheim/Rings households got together for hikes, picnics, parties, and neighborly chats. Myrt always had a colorful array of flowers growing in her yard, including peonies, poppies, and horsemint. In addition, each spring she and family members tilled the garden plot down the hill from the house and planted their vegetable garden. We tried to time our visits to Myrt's when her large lilac bush was in bloom, or when her rhubarb, carrots, onions, or peas were ready for harvesting. One of our favorite pastimes was sitting around the dining room table at The Ol' Timer playing a game or two of pinochle, then listening attentively to Myrt as she shared her rememberings. During one of these visits she began to talk of the Tregay family and its history:

When we finally knocked on Myrt's door, we got a warm welcome. "Come again," she said. And we did.

My mother, Gertrude LeFever, was working at a hotel in Nederland, Colorado, in the late 1800's when she met and married my father, Tom Tregay. Dad was a wagon driver at the time. The folks always referred to their first home as the "brown house." It was up Ellsworth Gulch close to the Iron Cross Mine. Dad got a job at the Iron Cross which, at the time, was owned by a Dr. Barrett, whose wife was a nurse. Two of my brothers, Tom Jr. and Pete, were born in the "brown house." The family moved for a short time to Chicago Creek over by Idaho Springs, where I was

Gertrude LeFever Tregay

The Iron Cross Mine still stands on the hillside southeast of the cabin. The building was renovated around 1980 when this photo was taken.

born on July 3, 1893. When I was two weeks old, the family moved back to Gilpin, and this time they lived in a little house which stood right across the fence south of our present cabin. My Mom often told the story of how it was here that "my baby Myrt almost lost her life." Mother had put me on the bed and covered me with a big comforter that my grandma had made. A furious windstorm shook the roof so hard that plaster and boards came down onto my bed. The comforter blew up over my head before the debris covered me. Mom would always end the story by saying, "That comforter was all that saved my baby."

The next move was to a house which stood below what is now the Molly Ball property. I think there had been a village called Sonora in that area. Molly remembers hearing of a hotel which had been in the meadow in front of their cottage, so it must have been some kind of a settlement at one time.

Brothers and sisters born after me were Pearl, Nettie, Alice, and Bill. Walter died when he was a baby and was buried in the cemetery on Dory Hill above Blackhawk.

I learned from Myrt that her father Tom had taken a liking to the area around Gilpin and decided to homestead a 320 acre plot. The Tregay homestead extended from what is now Snowline Subdivision up the hillside west to the meadow that was later Fort Cody. He built his homestead house just west of the old peat bog which is now Snowline Lake. His only help with the building project was a man "who could fall asleep in the middle of a carpenter job." The Tregays lived on the homestead ranch till most of the children were grown. Myrt's mother, who was known in the community as Grandma Tregay, was a big-hearted woman. She took in boarders, especially the various Gilpin school teachers, and housed and fed any stray who needed a place to stay. Henry Niccum, the town character, was often a guest in the Tregay home. Myrt remembers how Henry would come down from the hills with his crystalized rocks and say to her father, "Tom, see that gold?" Tom would look at it and reply, "Aw, that ain't no good," and throw it out the door. This would crush Henry.

The Tregay homestead around 1927. The little building (R) was over a spring. The pump remains.

He'd hang his head and go off to sulk. Henry was good to Myrt. When she was sick he'd take care of her. Grandma Tregay would say, "That's okay. Let him take care of her. We'll take care of him when he's sick." And they always did. Years later Grandma Tregay gave him her old kitchen cook stove to haul up to his Fourth of July Park. As heavy as those kitchen ranges are, I've often wondered how he ever got that thing up the mountain.

Tom and Grandma Tregay, 1930's.

When Harry Merchant and his friend George Knudson first arrived in Gilpin to try their hands at mining, there was no place for them to stay. The Tregay home was full of boarders at that time, but Grandma loaned them blankets and invited them to sleep in the haymow. Harry used to tell how he awakened in the night shivering from the cold and found that his blanket had been removed. Looking around, he discovered that the Tregay cow was making a meal of his covering. Fortunately, there was a foot or two of blanket still hanging from the cow's mouth. Harry woke George, and the two of them managed to extract the cover, which by now was a wet and slimy mess.

Another boarder was Maurine Miller, who came to teach at the one-room school in the Gilpin meadow. Maurine taught some of the Tregay children, but her teaching career was short, as Harry Merchant whisked her off to be his bride.

Gertrude Tregay was a hard worker and at one time ran the boarding house which was across the road from Jesse Williams' cabin, Snowcrest.

Sometimes the Tregay children would play around the boarding house while their mother was cooking. Myrt had a vivid memory of an incident that happened while she and her brother Tom were playing there. She told me this story one afternoon as she sat on the green couch in The Ol' Timer living

Very young Maurine and Harry Merchant.

room. She leaned forward and said, "See these fingers? I'm lucky to have them." I pulled my chair up close to have a look and to listen to another good Myrt tale.

Tommy, my oldest brother, and I were playing in back of the old boarding house where Mom was cooking. Tommy was chopping wood on a stump, just playing around, and I was pushing little pieces of wood down the holes that the ants had chewed in the stump. Tommy said, "If you don't keep your hand away from here, I'll chop your fingers off." I come in with my stick just as he come down with the ax, and it took this finger off and part of this one. You can see the scars there. They took me into Blackhawk. My Uncle Ike Tregay had a one-horse buggy, and him and Mom took me and my fingers in to the doctor. The doctor sewed the fingers back on, and they told me if I didn't cry they'd give me a marble. I didn't cry and they got me a big beautiful marble. When I got home, my other brother Pete, next to me in age, said he wanted to see what was inside of that marble, so he took the ax and broke the marble. Then I did cry, but it didn't do no good.

Pete and Tom were the main characters in another Tregay tale. This story could be called, "A Hole in One," or better still, "One in a Hole." Myrt loved telling this one:

Pete and Tom had a pet pigeon. One day it got away and flew into the open door of the outhouse. At that time their outhouse didn't have separate holes for seats, only a bar across a wide opening. The pigeon flew down into the pit and couldn't get out. The boys couldn't leave their pet pigeon to such a fate, so Tom, the older and larger of the two said, "Pete, you keep hold of me so I can reach down and pull that pigeon out. Pete took hold of Tom's feet and started to lower him into the hole, but Tom was too heavy, and Pete let go. The pigeon flew out and Tom climbed out after it, looking pretty awful. "Damn you, Pete. I told you to hold me." "I 'holed' you didn't I, Tommy?" and Tom said, "Yes, you 'holed' me when you let me go." Myrt said her mother had to laugh when the children told her what had happened.

The youngest son, Bill, was full of mischief and loved to play tricks on people. There was a fellow named Billy Huffman who worked on the Tregay ranch, and after a hard day of dirty work, he liked to bathe in the big horse tank up in the woods. Bill got the idea to wire the tank for an electric charge. When Billy got in the tank for his evening bath, Bill touched the wires to the battery and Billy shot straight up in the air. He didn't stop to get dressed; he just took off after Bill in his birthday suit and chased him all over the place.

Myrt was still living at home when Berger Nerheim came to Colorado from his home in Norway. He thought he'd try his hand at mining, and someone told him Gilpin was a good place to start. He took a shine to Myrt, but Myrt wasn't especially impressed. She was a beauty and could afford to be particular. As she said when we were looking at photos one day and I commented on her youthful good looks, "Yea, I had 'em all beat." One day Myrt went with her sister Nettie down to Denver to meet Nettie's husband and visit Auntie Morgans, Gertrude's sister. Berger followed her down, stopping in Boulder for a wedding dress, license, and ring. When he appeared at Auntie's door and proposed, Myrt was so flustered she didn't know what to do. She tried to get her aunt to advise her, but the wise old woman refused, saying, "This is one you gotta figure out for yourself." Myrt didn't have the heart to say, "No," after he'd gone to all that trouble, so she consented, and they were married on Christmas Day, 1918. They moved into a house up Beaver Creek by the mill, and Berger worked at various mines. He was having some health problems, so they moved to Denver, where he took up his former trades of carpenter and shoemaker. He also worked for Mr. Moffat of the Moffat Railroad, upholstering cars. The family still has some of the beautiful upholstering material that went into Mr. Moffat's private car.

Daughters Betty and Helen were born while the Nerheims lived in Denver, but when Helen was three years old and Betty was one, the family moved back to Gilpin. They lived in a house on the property that later became Jim Murray's building site and is now the Hamilton cabin. Later, Myrt's mother gave them the house across the street, next to the boarding house, and Berger, with his carpenter skills, made it into a nice four-room house.

Berger Nerheim with daughter Helen.

One day while Berger was working at The Smuggler Mine up Travis Gulch, a water hose broke and he got soaked. It had been snowing all day, and it got so deep that he couldn't get home, so he lay down by the boiler and went to sleep. He wakened with a chill which turned into pneumonia, and he died soon after, on January 29, 1929. He was 37 years old.

The cabin on the right was a wedding gift from Grandma Tregay to Myrt and Berger Nerheim. It stood next to the boarding house in the Gilpin town site.

After Berger's death, Myrt took the girls to live in California for awhile, but they were all so homesick that Myrt decided, "I'm gonna take me and my kids and go home."

Myrt's father, Tom, had died two weeks after Berger's death, and Grandma Tregay had moved to Boulder. Myrt and the girls returned to Colorado and lived with her for about a year and a half, and Myrt worked for a lady on University Hill. She and the girls still missed their mountains, so Myrt got a job in Perigo, up Gamble Gulch, cooking for the miners. Betty and Helen were the only kids in Perigo, and the miners were very good to them. They walked over the hill to school in Gilpin, the same one-room school that Myrt and all her brothers and sisters had attended. Teachers they remembered were Edna Lockner, Jean McKinstry, and Pearl Robb. From Perigo, it was back to Lump Gulch to a cabin just below the home that Cashions now own. In 1936, Myrt sold that place to the Merchants, and she and the two girls started building the present Nerheim cabin. The three of them did most of the building themselves, with a little help from Newt Neversetter, a one-armed carpenter who lived in Gilpin. It took three years to finish their new home. They mixed and poured the concrete for the foundation, put the logs in place, and did their own roofing. Helen was afraid of heights but got on the roof anyway, holding onto a rope and the nails with one hand and doing the hammering with the other. Betty, on the other hand, ran all over the roof without a thought of falling.

Some have told us that The Ol' Timer, then Snowcrest, the Williams home, had been built by Jesse Williams in the early 1880's. Others have given the date of 1893. By the time Betty and Helen remember anything about it, the elderly Mrs. Williams, Miranda, and her daughter Snow lived in it alone, and Snow was already a white-haired woman. We don't know if Jesse had died or moved somewhere else. Mrs. Williams was sick and in bed most of the time. The bed was where our living room couch sits. A curtain which hung where our front bedroom partition is now separated their living room/bedroom from the storage area, which is now our front bedroom. Snow would invite the girls in as they returned from school and ask them to entertain her mother and her. The girls would step from behind the curtain and recite poems and put on plays they'd learned at school. Then Snow would wind up the old phonograph, which Helen said was the same one we still have at the The Ol' Timer, and play recordings of Madame Schumanheink. We still have one of those recordings in the storage case of that old phonograph.

Snow's brother, Ernest Leroy, nicknamed Pet, was a lawyer in Denver. He owned and lived in the cabin behind Snowcrest. It had been built by Jesse's brother, Jonathan, about the same time that Jesse built Snowcrest. Myrt's daughter Betty liked to tell about Pet and his generous nature:

> *Pet had a huge Cadillac and would drive up to the cabin in this limousine and take us, the whole family, to the city for a treat. We'd go to Elich's Gardens, do the rides, eat ourselves sick, and come home the happiest bunch you ever saw.*

The lake which is listed on the Gilpin map as Laura Lake was on property that belonged to Pet, so it was known as Williams Lake. In the winter all the kids would go skating on it. They'd build bonfires on the bank to keep warm. It was a shallow lake and not dangerous, but there was a warm spring at one end, and the ice never froze solid. Betty remembered, "We were too dumb to stay away from it. There wasn't one of us that didn't fall in that lake. At least we got our feet clean," she laughed. "We'd wade out and run home to change clothes and be ready to go again, but Mom'd say, 'Oh, no you don't.'"

Esther in front of the Brinkerhoff shed.

57

Myrt and the girls loved nature and the wild animals in the woods—the deer, coyotes, foxes, and an occasional bear or mountain lion. One day Myrt was down by the old Brinkerhauf place picking huckleberries. She told me,

> *I was down on my knees pickin' those little berries when I heard a funny*
> *grunting and stomping noise. I looked up and here's this bear. He's standing up on*
> *his hind legs. I stood up and said, "Oh, you purdy thing," and he dropped down on*
> *all fours and ambled away. I followed him but lost him in the woods. I went back to*
> *the house and told Betty, and we both went looking for him, but he was long gone.*

Newt Neversetter
assisted Myrt,
Helen, and Betty
when they built their
mountain home.

Helen and Betty like to tell how old Newt Neversetter fooled the Forest Rangers. Newt, the one-armed carpenter who helped them when they were building their cabin, lived in the tin house just back of the boarding house. You can still see its remains lying on its side down by the creek. It was originally a log house and was on government land. Buildings on government land couldn't be changed or improved without permission from the Forest Service. Newt wanted to tear the log house down and build a new one, but the Forest Rangers wouldn't give him permission. After several tries, and refusals, Newt got a better idea. He went back to the agency and asked, "Could I just put some new siding on those old logs?" The government granted this request, and Newt went to work building a sturdy corregated tin structure around the outside of the logs. The next winter he dismantled the logs from the inside and used them for firewood.

Myrt had a "rememberer" that must have stored the names of every person and place she'd ever known. One day I was asking her to describe the town site of Gilpin from her first memories. She asked for paper and pencil and began to create a map of the buildings, stores, and homes, adding the names of the people who owned or operated them. You'll find this historic treasure at the end of the chapter.

On another summer day, Marj, Robert, Myrt, Helen, Bonnie Merchant Cashion, and I piled into Toho and drove up past the War Eagle Mine, around the bend to the Big Gold Dirt, and on to the Comstock Mines where Myrt's father had made his biggest profits from mining. In spite of her 88 years, Myrt wanted to hike up the trail to show everyone more mines. She could name them all and had stories to tell. It was a warm afternoon, and the rest of us were ready to return to the car, but Myrt said, "I just want to find one specific mine." Sure enough, when she reached the top of the hill where we could look down into Gamble Gulch, she pointed to the remains of a large operation. "This is the mine I was looking for," she said triumphantly. We drove on over into Gamble, and Myrt was able to bring that Gulch back to life by describing the old blacksmith shop, the grocery, the liquor store, the stables, and the remains of the old boarding house. She said, " I remember a tombstone up on the side of that hill. It was someone by the name of Moon, so I guess Moon Gulch might have been named after them. I'd like to go see if I could find it." The hill was steep, and Myrt did need a little help on this one. I took her hand and pulled, and Robert gently pushed her from behind, and we made it up that hill. With a little searching we found the gravesite she had remembered.

Although Myrt was having some difficulty with her hearing, there was nothing wrong with her eyesight. She could see wild strawberries or the tiny purple berries nestled in the huckleberry bushes better than any of us could, and she could still bend almost double to pick them.

During the winter of 1983, Myrt had a bad fall. She insisted she was okay, but her family called an ambulance and she was taken to a hospital for x-rays. She had broken her hip. We were afraid that she wouldn't be able to return to her mountain home, but by the following summer she was back, walking with a cane, but happy to be "where she belonged." She kept her hands busy with her fancy handwork and enjoyed visiting with family and friends. She even joined in a game or two of pinochle at The Ol' Timer. That was her last summer at her cabin. After a short illness, she died in the fall of that year.

The cabin remains in her family. Both Betty and Helen have joined their parents in "the next place." Betty's daughter, Betty Ann Huntsman Palmer, now owns the cabin and is making improvements, ever mindful of preserving its history, its treasures, and its stories.

Betty Ann and husband Don have two daughters, Deanna and Kathy. Last summer Betty Ann brought Kathy and her new baby Andrew to The Ol' Timer for a visit. As I was admiring little Andrew, it occurred to me that I was beginning a friendship with a 6th generation Tregay. Later, I got to wondering, " How many generations of the Tregay/Nerheim/Huntsman offspring will continue to be a part of this gulch, enjoying the family cabin, sharing its history, and passing on stories told by Myrt Tregay Nerheim, the "Lump Gulch Original."

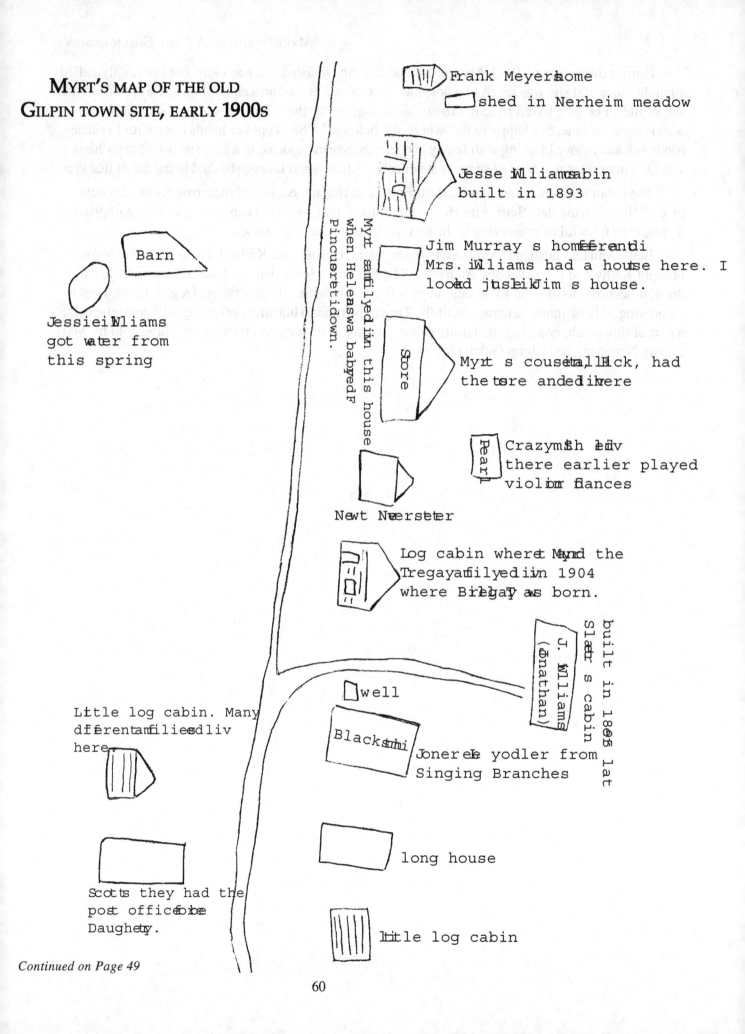

Frank Meyer home

shed in Nerheim meadow

Jesse Williams cabin
built in 1893

Jim Murray's home before and
Mrs. Williams had a house here. I
looked just like Jim's house.

Myrt and I lived in this house
when Helen was a baby and
Pincus retired down.

Store

Myrt's cousin, Wallick, had
the store and lived here

Pearl

Crazy Irish widow
there earlier played
violin for dances

Newt Nerseter

Log cabin where Myrt and the
Tregay family lived in 1904
where Birdie Tregay was born.

Barn

Jessie Williams
got water from
this spring

J. Williams
(Jonathan)

Slater's cabin
built in 1895 lat

Blacksmith

Joner the yodler from
Singing Branches

well

Little log cabin. Many
different families did live
here.

long house

Scotts they had the
post office before
Daughety.

little log cabin

Continued on Page 49

60

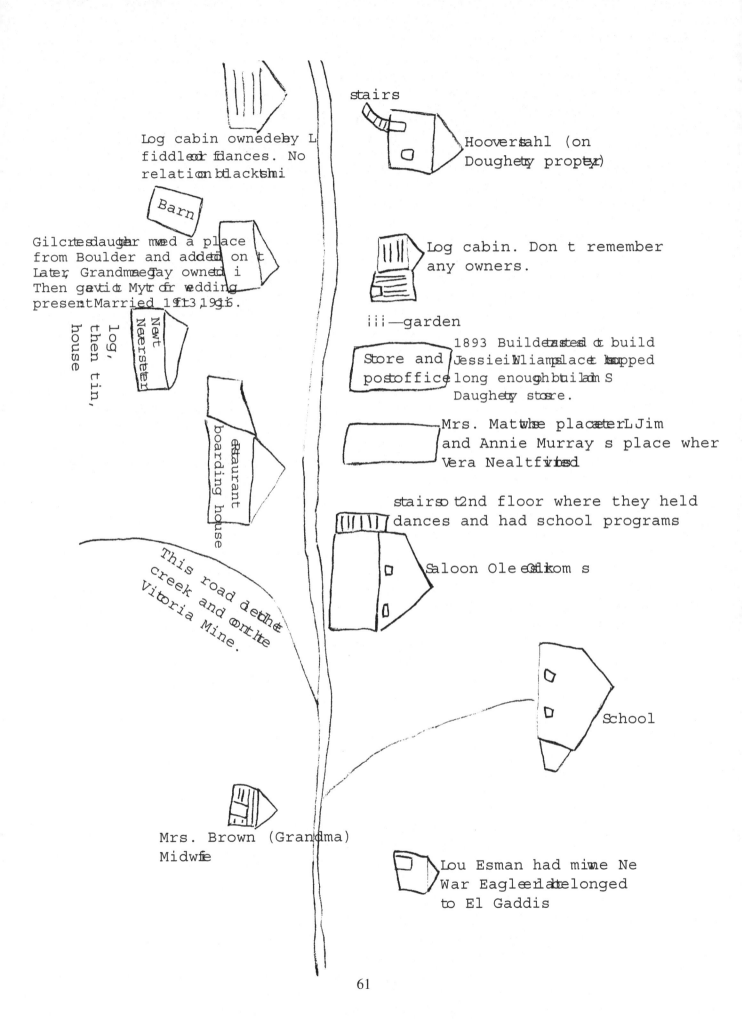

Log cabin owned by L
fiddled for dances. No
relation blacksmi

Barn

Gilcrests daughter moved a place
from Boulder and added on t
Later, Grandma Jay owned i
Then gave it to Myrt for wedding
present Married 1913, 1916.

log, then tin, house

Newt Neerster

Restaurant boarding house

This road de the creek and on the Vitoria Mine.

stairs

Hoover stahl (on Dougherty property)

Log cabin. Don t remember any owners.

iii—garden

Store and post office

1893 Builder started to build Jessie Williams place but stopped long enough to build in S Dougherty store.

Mrs. Matthew the place L Jim and Annie Murray s place where Vera Neal lived

stairs to 2nd floor where they held dances and had school programs

Saloon Ole Gilkom s

School

Mrs. Brown (Grandma) Midwife

Lou Esman had mine Ne War Eagle belonged to El Gaddis

MYRT NERHEIM, A LUMP GULCH ORIGINAL

Newt Neversetter's tin house down by the creek on the south side of Lump Gulch Road.

Myrt says, "See these fingers? I'm lucky to have them."

"That's it! That's the mine I was looking for."

Myrt and daughter Betty in front of their mountain home.

Three generations: Helen Nerheim Kindler, Myrt Nerheim, BettyAnn Huntsman Palmer, Betty Nerheim Huntsman, Betty Ann's children, Kathy and Deanna Palmer.

THE SUMMER OF SEVENTY GUESTS

The reader is not expected to keep all of these people and events straight. It's not important that you make all the connections. The purpose of this chapter is to give you, the reader, an idea of the variety of people and activities that were, and are, typical of most any summer at The Ol' Timer.

There would have been no way to reconstruct the summer of 1966 if my sister-in-law Nell hadn't saved the letter in which I described the activities at the cabin. Brother Glen and wife Nell had been our first guests early in June. When they arrived, we were in the middle of painting the sheet rock ceilings, which, in the twelve years we'd had the cabin, had never been painted. While we were in a mess anyway, we decided to put wooden lath stripping over the quarter-inch cracks between the rough ten inch boards that covered the logs and made up the kitchen walls. Once that was done, the walls needed a fresh coat of paint. Our guests pitched in and helped, and within a day or two we had the place looking good, by our standards.

After a week with us, Glen and Nell left to visit relatives in Arizona and wrote us about their beautiful trip. The summer was over, and we were back in Kansas before I settled down to writing a reply.

Dear Glen and Nell,

We enjoyed your letter and the description of Silverton and Ouray. It made us want to pack up and follow in your tracks, but when you read this brief account of our summer, you'll know why that was out of the question.

As I recall, you left on a Thursday morning, and our next week was to be a quiet one with no company expected. We had decided it would be a good time for our friend, Jeanette Wickstrom, from Gold Hill, to come spend a few days at The Ol' Timer. We called and made arrangements, and on Monday she and four of her Gold Hill friends came to spend the day, and Jeanette brought her suitcase. We wanted the Tolbert family, [our Kansas friends who were spending the summer at Blue Spruce] to meet the Gold Hill gang, so we had invited them up to share our simple stew dinner in the evening. This would make a cozy thirteen. When we stopped at LeZotte's grocery in Rollinsville after a tour of the countryside, Ray, the owner, informed us that an Emporia teacher friend, Marge Kelley, whom we had invited earlier, and who had thought she couldn't come, was on her way from Central City. [We didn't have a phone at the cabin, so our friends, the LeZottes, who owned and operated the grocery store, were our connection with the outside world.] Well, what's fourteen when you're cooking for thirteen? When Marge arrived, we found that her in-laws and their son had brought her, and since they seemed bewildered as to what to do and where to eat, we invited them to stay for dinner, which they did. We kept running to the kitchen to add various kinds of juice to the stew, and seventeen of us sat down to a very liquid stew. The camaraderie was good, and we had a delightful evening.

Meanwhile, Betty Campbell [with whom I was sharing the cabin] *had heard from a cousin and friend who had planned to do the races in Denver. The races had been postponed due to flood conditions, so while they were in the area they thought they'd just stop up and visit us for a couple of days. They are two fun gals, and we were glad that they were coming. They arrived on Tuesday morning, and our party now consisted of Jeanette, Marge Kelly from Emporia, and Betty's cousin and friend. We all took Jeanette back to Gold Hill on Wednesday, taking the day to explore and sightsee. Jeanette said she'd never had such a time, whatever that meant.*

In the meantime, Betty had received a letter from her sister and family in Kansas City. Their trip to California had been cancelled, so they would come to the cabin instead. They and their camper arrived Thursday A.M, five of them. Betty's cousin and friend had left, Marge Kelley was still with us, and we were back to a nice little group of eight, except when we had the Tolberts up, making it fourteen.

Marge Kelley left Friday evening—oh, I forgot to mention that one evening during the week of Jeanette's visit, we were just sitting down to more watered down something-or-other when there came a tap, tap, tap at the door. Some friends of Jeanette had learned that she was visiting us and stopped in to visit her, delaying our dinner by an hour or so. The next night when our group of fourteen was seated for a song-fest, Mert and Howard Knoll, you know, my Ye Olde Fashioned boss and husband, came to spend the evening and see if I didn't want to work in my spare time.

Back to Marge leaving on Friday. That left only Betty's sister and family till the next Tuesday. When they left we were down to two. Meanwhile I had heard from [niece] *Carol, saying that if it was O.K., she and Jan would drive out with the four kids* [Carol's three and Jan's one] *to be with us during the second week of Marj and Robert's vacation. We spent the rest of that week, Tuesday through Saturday, getting ready for the next batch.*

Marj, Robert, and their friends, Charles and Doris Sheetz, arrived Saturday evening after much detouring around the flooded areas of Denver. Our friends, the Taliaferros, from El Dorado, were spending the weekend at the Alpine Motel in Rollinsville, and we had them up for the day on Sunday. Tolberts came up Sunday evening for a sing-along.

It had rained so much that we couldn't get in and out of our driveway, so Sunday P.M. the men in the group went out to make a rock bridge. "Nature boy" Robert rolled a large rock onto his big toe, and by Monday the toe was red and swollen and painful, so we took him to Boulder to the doctor. They drilled into his toenail to remove the pressure, and it began to improve, but Robert didn't do any hiking those two weeks.

66

Tuesday we went to Georgetown and got a few prize purchases at the antique shops. It rained most of the day, and when we got home the roof in the back room was leaking. Wednesday we worked on the roof and took a trip to Gold Hill. We were going to come back by the old Switzerland Trail road, but Doris got a bad headache, so we went home the fastest route and put her to bed. Mary Tolbert's parents came to visit them that day, so we had the six Tolberts and her parents up for another sing-along. Doris slept through it all.

Thursday, Betty and Charles built a wooden bridge so we could get our cars in and out of the driveway, and we all went up Eldora to Helm Falls. Charles had got overheated from working in the sun, so we brought him home and put him to bed. He recovered quickly, and Doris was feeling better, so the two couples did Central City in the evening while Betty and I stayed home and paid our overdue bills.

Friday it continued to rain, and in the evening the lights went out. We lit every candle in the place, built up the fires, popped corn in the old iron skillet on the kitchen range, and played Wahoo. We thought it was great fun. Saturday we went as far as Boulder with Doris and Charles as they headed for home. We shopped and messed around, then went to spend the evening with some new friends, Pat and Bill Kitchen, and their three kids. Carol, Jan and company arrived at about ten P.M., and the kids were excited about the mountains and the cabin.

Brad got a little out of control one day, and Marj said, "Brad, we need your cooperation." Brad said, "You had it, did you lose it again?" Living with Robert is not doing that child any good.

Well, needless to say, we had a wild time with that bunch. Sunday the five Kitchens came up, June and Chic arrived, [sister and husband] *and Marj got sick and took to her bed. I told her I knew how she felt when Mom was in the hospital during her last illness, and all was confusion at Marj's house with family coming and going. Marj said, "How could Mom start all this mess and then go off and leave us?"*

While the kids were at the cabin from Saturday night to Thursday A.M., we took them gold mining, went to Brainard Lake and hiked to Long Lake and Lake Isabelle, did Central City, shopped in Boulder, and joined the Tolberts for a picnic up Flagstaff mountain. Carol, Jan, and the children drove back to Kansas, leaving on Thursday morning, and Robert and Marj got reservations on the train for their Friday night trip back to Kansas.

Thursday, Marj, Robert, Betty and I went over the Gap Road and later explored an old mine. We came home with so many pretty rocks, mostly iron pyrite, that we said we thought we might start a rock shop. Robert said, "Why don't you call it the "ore" house?"

The last day of the family visit is almost too complicated to relate. Chic had to take his car to Boulder, and since June didn't want to sit around a garage, she went with us while we took the Switzerland Trail road. In the middle of nowhere, we hit a rock which bounced up into an almost impossible place and jammed the emergency brake so that we couldn't get it off. We crept with brake dragging into Boulder, sat in the garage while they fixed it, and barely got Marj and Robert back in time for them to pack and get to the train for their return to Kansas.

I'm tired, and I'm sure you are, so I'll grind to a halt. The next two weeks were full of work and play. We left for Kansas late afternoon on Friday and arrived home at three A.M. Saturday. We think we will never be young enough again to stand such a vacation, but truthfully, we had a wonderful summer.

Love,
Sister Esther

Later, when we were figuring the number of people who had either had a meal with us or stayed overnight, we counted seventy summer guests. The next summer we altered our policy of "You all come." But not much.

HENRY NICCUM

Henry Niccum was the perfect example of a town character. Back in the early 1900's, he lived in various shacks in the hills around Gilpin, up Lump Gulch. Lump Gulch had acquired its name during the gold rush days when a number of good sized lumps, or nuggets, had been panned from its stream. Henry hadn't been gone from Lump Gulch long when I bought my cabin in the old town site in 1953. The old timers were still spinning yarns about his interesting and irregular behavior.

People who had actually known Henry agreed that he looked like the Happy Hooligan character in the comic strips. He wore an old bowler hat, was quite short, and as one old timer put it, "His face was so wrinkled, he could just screw his hat right onto his head. Like a prune, he was." Henry was hard of hearing, so whenever you'd speak to him he'd cup his hand over his ear and say, "Eh?" He seldom caught the drift of a conversation. George Merchant, who grew up in Lump Gulch, recalls: "One day my father, Harry, was working at his drawing board which he had set up in the back room of our cabin. Henry came to the front door and asked, 'Where's Harry?' Mother replied, 'He's busy working.' 'Eh?' says Henry. 'He's working,' repeated mother in a louder voice. 'Oh, in bed, eh?' Mom just let it go at that."

Henry Niccum and mules. He liked to show this photo and say, "I'm the one on the left."

Henry spent a good deal of his time digging prospect holes and was always carrying around rocks from his diggings. He'd spit on them, polish them on his sleeve, show them to anyone who'd give him a minute, and say, "Look at that gold." Because he never actually made any money from his mining, he was not above asking for a handout. "Gertie, have yuh got a cup u' coffee?" or "Myrt, what's fer dinner?" He not only scrounged food but also tools or dynamite—whatever he could get his hands on to help him dig for his gold. George also tells of the time when Henry got hold of a couple or three sticks of dynamite and took them home for safe keeping. "He always figured somebody was going to rob him, so he hid the dynamite in the kitchen stove. He figured no one would look there. He went off to Rollinsville or Central City or somewhere and was gone for quite awhile. By the time he returned, he'd forgot about the dynamite and went to cook his supper. He lit the stove and went outside to get a bucket of water, and WHAMMY, the stove exploded. It knocked one wall out of his cabin. It also scared poor Henry to death and he came running down to Gilpin hollering, 'Somebody's trying to kill me!'"

Molly Ball, who spent summers in her cottage up the road from The Ol' Timer beginning in 1928, loved to tell this story: "It seems that Henry came walking down the main street of Gilpin in the midst of a big snow storm. There was about a two foot accumulation on the ground, and Henry was laboriously trudging along. In his tracks, close behind, followed a mountain lion. According to the story, several of the residents of the village got up on their roofs to watch the show. Henry was apparently unaware for some time that he was being followed, but suddenly his steps grew faster and longer, and so did the lion's." The only trouble with that story is that we don't know what happened next.

We do know that Henry lived to a ripe old age—old enough to have a good many years enjoying his old-age pension. Since he had never made a dime from his mining, the pension allowed him a life style he'd never known. Our friend Helen Nerheim Kindler, who grew up in Gilpin, remembers: "With his first check he went to town and bought himself a new suit and hat. It was the first decent clothes anyone had ever seen him in. He was so proud. From then on, whenever he'd get a check, he'd head for Rollinsville for groceries. He'd always buy a big sack of candy and walk back home eating piece after piece. Whatever was left after he got to Gilpin, he'd bring to my sister Betty and me."

Our own favorite Niccum story was the one about Henry's Fourth of July picnic ground. Henry had a mining claim high on Lindeman Peak, also called Fairburn Mountain. It was in a high meadow surrounded by aspen and evergreens. To him the beauty of it was overwhelming and he felt a need to share it. Being a patriotic sort, he hit on the idea of a Henry Niccum Fourth of July Park. In his mind he could see neighbors from all over Lump Gulch coming to celebrate that occasion, sharing in the beauty of those surroundings. He went to work to construct picnic tables and benches attached to a circle of trees. He built a cupboard on the side of a Colorado Spruce, hauled up an old kitchen stove given to him by Grandma Tregay, and whitewashed the base of the trees in preparation for his Fourth of July picnic. Some said he neglected one important detail. He never got around to inviting his guests. Others thought that no one could find the place, or perhaps no one wanted to join him in his Fourth of July celebration. Whatever the case, the story goes that each year he gave his trees a fresh coat of whitewash, and each year no one came.

This story intrigued and saddened us. Poor Henry had never realized his kind and generous dream. We began to search for the spot but each time came home disappointed. On a summer hike after we had given up ever finding it, we came upon some trees with the remains of boards nailed to them. In the middle of them was what was left of an old cook stove. Then we spotted the beat-up washtub with hardened whitewash and something we could imagine had been a cupboard on the side of a tree. It had to be. We'd found it! Henry's Park.

We could not let this legend die without a happy ending. That Fourth of July, 1977, and each year since, we have honored Henry's wish for a big celebration. Old timers and new, we pile food, blankets, and tables into four-wheel drives and make our pilgrimage to Henry's Park. Carvings in a large aspen tree attest to each year's participants. Each year a flag or patriotic emblem is placed high in the tree. There is the singing of patriotic songs, and there are stories of Henry, the town character, as reviewed by the old timers.

On the Fourth of July, 1981, an old man wandered into the picnic ground just as we were filling our plates and asked, "Is this the Catholic/Presbyterian picnic?" When we said it wasn't, he cupped his hand over his ear and said, "Eh?" When we asked if he could use a bite to eat, he eagerly heaped his plate. Was this the ghost of Henry come at last to enjoy a dream fulfilled? We were delighted to learn as we visited, that, though he was not Henry's ghost, he had been Henry Niccum's mining partner at one time. He had even lived with Henry in his old shack on this very mountain. John Holcup was his name, and he had recently returned from years in California. He was back looking to buy a piece of land and renew his interest in prospecting. As we visited, it seemed that I was spending the Fourth of

July with Henry at his mountain park, talking about the good old days, watching him cup his hand over his ear to catch what I was saying, seeing his eyes dance at the thought of food, or drink, or prospecting, or more important, this beautiful spot which bears his name.

In the summer of 1984, I wrote this song about Henry Niccum and his Fourth of July Park:

HENRY NICCUM

Old Henry Niccum built a park up on the mountain,
He fashioned it of boards and nails and whitewashed all the trees.
He made tables, he made benches and a cupboard for his dishes,
And hauled up an old stove that had been Grandmother Tregay's.

Chorus

Hey, Henry, tell us of your plan. Hey, Henry, tell us if you can,
Who you're having to your party, for it must be quite a gang.
"It's my Fourth of July, high in the sky, annual celebration, and it's going to be a bang."

Though his plan was quite delightful, Henry kept it very quiet,
He forgot to tell the neighborhood to join him in the fun.
Every year he sat and waited for his annual celebration,
Sat and waited from the dawn of day until the setting sun.

Chorus

Poor Henry, wasn't that a shame? Poor Henry, he kept on just the same,
With his plan to have a party mid the aspen and the pine.
Have his Fourth of July, high in the sky, annual celebration.
It was going to be a bang.

Henry died and left his park. He left his benches and his tables.
Left his tub with all its whitewash, and his cupboard on the tree.
It is rotting and decaying, but it tells a mighty story,
Of a man who loved his mountains, now he's Lump Gulch history.

Chorus

Hey, Henry, it wasn't such a shame.
Hey, Henry, you're now a man of fame,
For we like to have our picnics in the park that bears your name.
It's our Fourth of July, high in the sky, annual celebration,
And it truly is a bang, bang, bang, bang, Boom diddlee boom boom. Bang, bang.

For at least twenty years we gathered friends and family, often thirty or so, for a Fourth of July celebration. As some of the regulars began to find the trip too difficult, we had our picnics in the side yard of the cabin, and then those who wished to climbed into four-wheel drives for a visit to Henry's Park. I can't remember that there has been a summer since 1977 when we haven't taken some of our guests on this trip of historic importance. I must admit that Henry is not the only draw. The trip through the woods, and across the open meadow, is a sight of such beauty. The hillsides are literally covered with every kind of mountain wildflower. The columbine grow more profusely on those hills than anyplace I've ever seen them. The views of the Continental Divide to the west, and of the lake and settlement in the gulch below, are breathtaking. And there are the wild strawberries in season. Nephew Charley, the great elk hunter, got so wrapped up in berrying one summer that an elk walked past him a stone's throw distance, and he never noticed.

Because I love the beauty, the history, and the memories of this place, I am telling family members that I wish to have my ashes scattered among the flowers on the side of the road that leads to Henry's Park. But, I hasten to remind them," No hurry."

Henry Niccum

VERSE 1

Old   Henry   Niccum   built   a   park   up   on   the   mountain   He
fashioned   it of boards and   nails and white-washed all   the   trees. He made   tables,   he made   benches   and a
cupboard   for   his   dishes,   And   hauled up an   old stove   that had   been   Grandmother Tregay's

CHORUS 1

Hey,   Henry,   Tell   us   of   your plan Hey,   Henry   Tell   us   if   you   can   who   you're
having   to your   party,   for   it   must   be   quite a gang.   It's   my   4th of July,   high in the sky
begin verse 2
annual   celebration   and   it's   going to   be   a   bang.   Though   his

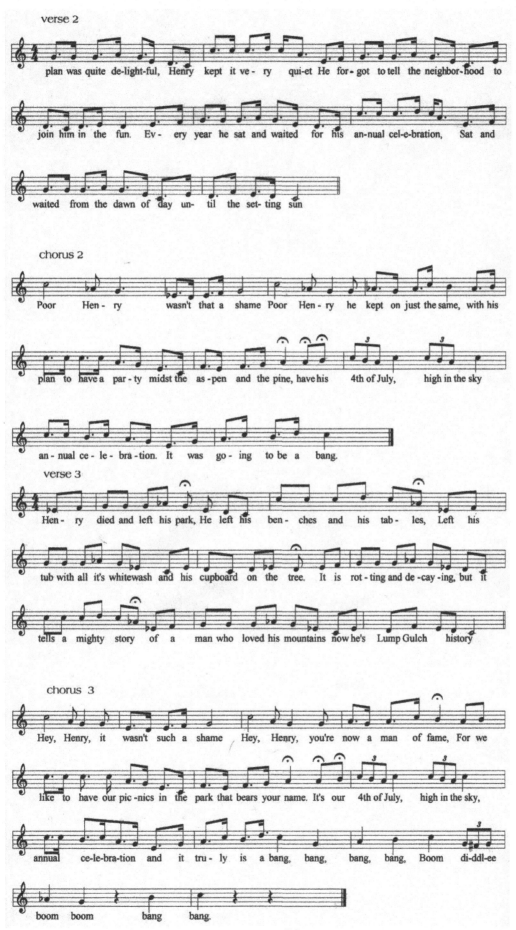

HENRY NICCUM

Esther at the remains of Henry's picnic tables.

Sally showing Henry's cupboard on the tree.

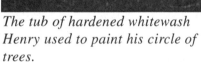

John Holcup, Henry's partner from mining days. "Is this the Catholic/Presbyterian picnic?"

The tub of hardened whitewash Henry used to paint his circle of trees.

Picnicking at Henry's Park.

July 4, 1986, Statue of Liberty celebration. "Sorry, Esther, the sheet doesn't quite do it."

THE NIGHT THE LAW CONVERGED ON THE STATUE

During the summer of 1984, I asked George Merchant, our neighbor down the road from the cabin, to retell his story about the law and the statue so that I could tape it for posterity. George had been an announcer for a Kansas radio station at one time. He had a rich resonance to his voice that enhanced any story, and this one, like all of his tales, was made better if you could sit with him by his Franklin fireplace in his Lump Gulch home and listen to him chuckle as he recalled each humorous incident. Still, this story can be enjoyed in any form, and so I will now transcribe it as it was told to me and the tape machine by George Merchant III.

Well, it seems like we had an armed robbery in the county one night. There were two or three fellows show up with ski masks and automatic weapons and robbed a neighbor down the road. They evidently didn't have a vehicle, as they took off down the road on foot. The neighbor called the sheriff's department, and the sheriff's department called out all the deputies and reserves to comb the area for these guys. I had a statue sitting out in my yard, life size. One of my sons had given it to me for a joke one Christmas, and we'd had a lot of fun with it. We named it Boris and used it as a decoration. We'd dress him up like Santa Claus at Christmas time, Uncle Sam on the Fourth of July, and this kind of thing. At the time of the robbery it was mid-winter, and we had Boris dressed in a ski mask and jacket, sitting up on a stump in the front yard. I've been on rescue patrol for a number of years and always have my radio band on for emergencies. When I heard the call on the radio about the robbery, I went out and turned on my outside lights. I knew if these guys were trying to hide they wouldn't be heading for some place where all the lights were on. Well, one of the deputies, John Starkey, came up the gulch. He knew where I lived, but he hadn't been to my place since I'd got the statue. He came around the corner and his headlights picked up Boris sitting in the yard with the ski mask on and he flat panicked. He got on the radio and started hollering for help, said he'd spotted one of those guys in George Merchant's yard, ski mask, brown jacket, the whole bit. The sheriff, Jim Benson, a good friend of mine, realized immediately what had happened. He started laughing and said, "You're looking at George's statue."

It took Jim a long time to live that one down. He told me later, he says, "Did you ever come around that corner there with your head down behind the dashboard?" At any rate, everyone in the county heard about it. I had quite a bit of traffic for awhile. Everybody was coming up to see what it looked like. I took a picture of it one day and sent it to Jim. He has it on his bedroom wall. We had a lot of fun with that incident, the night the law converged on the statue.

Boris, the Merchant's statue, dressed in ski mask and jacket

*A young George Merchant,
announcer for a Kansas radio station*

*George visiting with Myrt Nerheim at The Ol' Timer,
summer, 1979*

PRINCESS AND POPPY

"There they go again," I said to Merla as I sat in my wicker rocker looking out the large dining room window.

"Who's 'they'?" Merla questioned without looking up from her book.

"You know, the couple that strolls past here occasionally. She's wearing her broad-brimmed hat and gloves, and they're linked arm in arm. I wonder who they are, and where they live?" "Why don't you ask Jim?" That was Merla's way of saying, "Don't bother me. I'm reading."

It wasn't unusual for Merla to be reading and improving her mind while I sat observing my surroundings.

I took her suggestion to ask neighbor Jim about this couple, and he informed me: "That's Harry and Maurine Merchant. They live down the road toward the highway. You know where that garage sits by the road? Their house is up that path and into the lodgepole pine forest. They call their place Wits' End." Jim said they weren't much on neighboring, so we contented ourselves with observing them from our cabin window, noticing how they seemed to enjoy each other's company.

It wasn't until the mid-sixties, when I was teaching in Emporia in the winter and sharing the cabin with Betty Campbell in the summer, that we received a letter from Maurine with photos of The Ol' Timer taken after a heavy snowfall. She said she'd been prompted to write because she thought we might enjoy seeing our place dressed in its winter coat. We wrote a "thank you" note and said we'd like to meet them when we returned to Lump Gulch. The next summer after Betty and I had the cabin in shape, we walked down the road and up the path to Wits' End. We were greeted as if we were old friends, and that first visit was followed by years of shared celebrations.

Wits' End was especially inviting on chilly days. We'd sit by their fireplace sipping hot tea and munching goodies as we chatted. There were large windows on the north, south, and west, inviting nature to join them in their sitting room. Harry always called his wife "Princess," and she called Harry "Poppy" or "my dear husband."

This was the Maurine and Harry in the Myrt Nerheim story—Maurine who came to teach in the Gilpin one-room school, and Harry who had come to the area to check out mining interests.

These are some notes I jotted after having spent some time in their company:

Maurine is a grand lady in every way. She is attractive, witty, talented, and caring. She is a graduate of an

Maurine, an accomplished pianist, also played the violin.

Eastern finishing school for young women, and an accomplished pianist. It's hard to picture this refined woman coming west from Illinois in a covered wagon.

Harry Merchant is no ordinary person, either. He's Maurine's match in looks, humor, and intelligence. He was trained in mining and construction engineering, attending the School of Mines in Golden, Colorado. During the Depression he supervised the building of the CCC Camps all over Colorado, and when their only child George was born, Harry was supervising the construction of the Cosmopolitan Hotel in Denver.

During one of our times together, Betty asked what had brought them back to Lump Gulch to retire, and Harry responded:

While we were in Denver, we'd slip away on weekends and revisit our old Gilpin haunts. We had good memories of this place. In 1932 we bought an acre of land from Pete Peterson, who had a house across the road, and added another piece of land from Myrt Nerheim. On this property we built a rock house for our weekend get-away. After World War I Gilpin had pretty well died down, but Grandma Tregay was still around, and there was a small grocery store. Denny Sullivan, Ed Quinn, and George Murray, Jim's brother, were living in a lean-to off Sam Daugherty's old post office and store. There was Jake Hooverstall, who called himself the remittance man, and Johnny Eoff, who lived in the old Pet Williams' cabin.

Wits' End, the home the Merchant's built among the lodgepole pines.

The rock house was picturesque and served us very well for a time, but it held moisture and things mildewed. By 1948 we decided we wanted a more permanent structure, a place where we could retire. As we sat on a rocky knoll overlooking the road yet nestled among the lodgepole pines, we decided that this would be a perfect spot for our new place, "Wits' End." Newt Neversetter, the one-handed carpenter who helped built the Nerheim cabin, helped us get started with our building project. He and a man named Axel Roman built a one-room cabin up on stilts, and Maurine and I did the rest.

Newt was an interesting fellow. He had a hook attached to his stub, and people were amazed at what he could do with that hook. He had built silos, windmills, grain elevators, and cabins all over this part of the country. When Newt went fishing in the "crick," he didn't bother with a fishing pole. He'd just kneel down, put his hook in the water, and grab a fish.

Harry enjoyed reviewing his courtship with Maurine. When I asked him if he remembered their first date, he said, "The date started when I met her as she got down from the buggy at Tregay's, and it has never stopped."

He admitted that after that first meeting he had a hard time keeping his mind on his business. He and a companion, Jack Hummel, were working the No-Name mine, which was not far from the school where Maurine was teaching. Harry said, "Jack was down the ladder in the mine checking samples. I was on the surface running an Armstrong heist on a windlass, pulling up the samples. I'd get interested in the schoolhouse and what was going on there. Jack would holler, 'Hey, up there, get your mind off that school marm and watch what you're doing. You're kicking rocks down here.'"

The No-Name Mine in Gilpin, across from the old boarding house

We not only enjoyed our summer visits but also looked forward to hearing from Maurine in the winter. Her wit and way with words made her letters worth keeping. I'll share excerpts from one written in 1974:

Up in the Boondocks
Gilpin County
September 5, 1974

Dear, Dear Esther and Betty,

Your cheerful and interesting letter is enjoyed by each of us and we appreciate your writing to us UP-Gulch People! We do feel a little lonesome, knowing that you are not occupying The Ol' Timer...

We have not heard any more about the mountain lion. However, Mrs. Buxton vows that she saw it with her very own eyes and it was a GREAT BIG LION! I heard something padding around on the porch directly under my open window one moonlight night and when I cautiously peered out I saw a medium sized creature scratching itself on the porch rail. It must have been a raccoon. I would have felt distinguished if I had scared away a lion or a cougar with my sudden outburst of "SCAT-WHOOSH." We used to see bear tracks often in the back road, but not lately. Baby Doe, our neighbor-hood deer, was the most welcome visitor in the wildlife persuasion. Such a dear little friend. (Baby Doe was an orphaned baby deer that became a Lump Gulch pet. She is the deer Susan Tolbert is feeding in the story on Ceremonies and Celebrations.) *I imagine she is a favorite member of a herd up around Georgetown where she was transplanted by an official of the State Fish and Game Commission.* ("Baby" was transplanted after she made her way to Central City and was playing havoc with people's flower gardens.)

We took a little stroll over to Gamble Gulch a few days ago just to gaze at that magnificent view of Arapaho Peak and Corona Pass. Our old trail down the hill to that little cluster of cottages, Glynn Haven, is practically obliterated. Even the old blazes indicating, "To Rollinsville," and "To Gilpin," barely show where they were carved in those big pine trees. My dear husband and I used to walk down that way when we wanted to catch the train to Denver. When we arrived at the station we would inquire from the agent when the train was due, and his reply was invariably, "I don't have any idea when today's train will come through, but yesterday's train is due any minute." The conductor would always walk up and down the aisle of the passenger coach yelling, "Get your partners for the trip through the tunnel." The general practice was for the passengers to get out and help the crew roll the rocks off the tracks at frequent intervals. No kidding. Once in a while Mrs. Retallack, who carried the mail, would offer us a lift in her Model T Ford, but we were not spared the privilege of rolling big stones off the auto road. Mr. Grant Phillis had a car that stalled every few feet, and he would have to place a rock behind the rear wheel to keep the car from rolling backward while he went through examining every cause for the stall. Mr. Phillis was one of the remarkable characters in these parts. By his own admission he was an itinerant preacher and used the old schoolhouse to hold services for the Holy Roller's religious organization. He left the country for parts unknown. You have been told about Henry Niccum, I'm sure. I laugh when I recall his habit of stopping at Tregay's house to mooch a meal and would offer to chop wood or repair harness or storm doors. In ten minutes he would leave his job and walk to the next neighbor's. He was a replica of the old cartoon, Happy Hooligan. Once I put a tin can on his head and took a picture of him looking through an old discarded tire. He loved it….

At long last I will bring this young volume to a close and listen for your sigh of relief. Please do write to us again whenever you have time. Your communications are precious. We all regard you as our very best and most loved friends. Keep up your wonderful spirits and good health and we hope spring will hasten its arrival so you will return to our neighborhood.

With love from "Mere Chance," (Merchants)
Harry and Maurine

Our friendship continued through the years with birthday and Fourth of July celebrations, and much sharing of stories. The big celebration of the summer was always their anniversary dinner. It became their tradition to gather a group of family and friends together and treat us to steak and trout at Beaver Inn, a nice restaurant on the Wondervu road. Their sixty-second anniversary was our last big celebration.

An anniversary celebration at Beaver Inn.
L to R-Betty Campbell, George and Bonnie Merchant,
Harry and Maurine, Esther

A birthday party for Maurine at The Ol' Timer. Daughter-in-law Bonnie made fancy cakes.

Princess and Poppy were in their nineties when poor health forced them from Wits' End to a nursing home in Denver. They are now at rest, side by side, in the Gilpin Pioneer Cemetery nestled in the lodge-pole pine forest a "stone's throw" from Wits' End. Theirs was a love story from beginning to end.

THINKING OF BONNIE

"T'was her thinking of others that made you think of her."
Elizabeth Browning

The life story of Bonnie Merchant Cashion cannot be adequately described on paper, and especially in one short chapter. A book would still not do the job. It takes knowing Bonnie to realize the magnitude of her strength of character and her big-hearted personality. Still, I must do the best I can to include some of her story and share my impressions of this long-time friend.

Bonnie was born in Winnette, Montana, May 26, 1924. Her birth name is Weowna Lorraine. Her sister, Ella, eleven years old at the time, had a speech impediment and couldn't say Weowna so, since their mother's nickname was Blondie, Ella tried calling her baby sister Little Blondie. It sounded like she was saying Little Bonnie, and the name "Bonnie" stuck. The family moved to Chattanooga, Tennessee, and when Bonnie was three years old her mother enrolled her in kindergarten. Schools in Tennessee at that time had no laws determining enrollment age. The requirement was that children had to know the alphabet and recognize numbers. On her first day of school, Bonnie told the teacher her name was "Bonnie." The teacher asked for her middle initial and Bonnie said it was "L." In the South if your middle initial was "L," it was assumed that your middle name was "Lee." Thus Bonnie Lee was the name she assumed at school and has continued to use. Nicknames were not unusual in their family. Her father, Glen Grant Carter, went by the nickname "Happy," and her mother, Lazzetta Elizabeth O'Neil, was called "Blondie" because of her mass of blonde hair.

Bonnie took on family responsibilities early in life. Her father raised Appaloosa horses, training them for circus performance, but since he was also in the oil business and away from home for extended periods of time, he left Bonnie in charge of the hired hands. Her mother had diabetes which was gradually taking her eyesight, so Bonnie helped her mother in every way she could.

Bonnie's father was Mormon and her mother was Roman Catholic; Bonnie was raised in the Catholic faith. When she graduated from high school at age sixteen, she joined the Sisters of Mercy Convent in Stillwater, Oklahoma, and took nurses' training. Some of the beliefs of the convent didn't work for this independent thinker, so she left Sisters of Mercy and enlisted in the Army Nursing Corp. During World War II she was sent to Germany and Japan to care for prisoners of war. Bonnie cannot bring herself to share stories of this time. She says, "It was just too painful."

After the war she was offered a job with the American Red Cross and served that organization from headquarters in Kansas and Colorado. In Colorado she met and married George Merchant III, son of Maurine and George Harry Merchant II. George had just graduated from art school but soon took up a career as announcer for a radio station in Boulder.

The couple moved to a cabin in Evergreen, one which Bonnie had purchased earlier with money she'd saved while in the service. The cabin sat high on a hill above the town and lacked modern conveniences. The couple had no indoor plumbing or electricity, and their only source of heat was a wood-burning stove. This was the setting for the birth of their three children, George IV and twin sons Pat and Mike.

The family returned to Kansas for a time to assist with the care of Bonnie's parents. George was hired by station KSOK in Arkansas City and continued his career as radio announcer, giving himself the title "Lonesome George." In spite of a very busy schedule, Bonnie went to school at Kansas University and got her Bachelor's degree in social work.

Bonnie proved herself equal to any task the Red Cross had to offer, and when the George Merchant family moved back to Boulder, she became Regional Administrator for Boulder and Longmont. Later she was appointed to the position of Disaster Director for Colorado and Wyoming. Her territory extended West to Guam and North to Alaska, and she was in charge of rescue operations in many devastating situations—hurricanes, floods, fires, tornadoes. For a time she made her headquarters in a Western Colorado community so that she could attend college in Provo, Utah, where she received her Master's degree in social work.

Bonnie and George had purchased a piece of property on the Lump Gulch road across from his parents' home, Wits' End, in the late '50's . The building on the property was a structure that had been started by a DeMolay group from Denver, but the project had been abandoned before it was finished. In 1970 the Merchants began the work of turning the building into a home where they could live year-round. There was much to be done, and their creativity and know-how were put to the test. Bonnie was a "make-do" person. She papered the walls in the hallway with maps of the area and covered some of the kitchen walls with newspapers containing articles of historic interest. One wall of the kitchen was covered with boards rescued from old mines, mills, and abandoned buildings, each having the name of its original building-site burned into the wood.

Once Bonnie and George moved into "Merchants' Claim," as they named it, and became our neighbors, our times together were frequent. George introduced us to the natural world he had grown up in, sharing such things as bear claw marks high on aspen trees, the buckboard fence with the fairy slipper orchids, and the best spots for picking wild strawberries. We had evenings at The Ol' Timer with George strumming his guitar and singing ballads and work songs while Bonnie sat stitching or crocheting, feeding him the words to his songs when he forgot.

Along with all of Bonnie's other accomplishments and talents, she is a poet. Our Christmas letters from Merchants' Claim combined George's art work and Bonnie's poetry. She made me a gift of several examples of their combined artistic talents. One of my favorites is, "Homesick Heart":

HOMESICK HEART

These buildings are high as my mountains.
These cities more vast than my plains.
These skies are as heavy with smoke
As summer skies heralding rains.

Each roar of the trolleys is equaled
By the thunder of avalanche.
The brilliant lights of the Great White Way
Are kin to the lightning's blanche.

Like frightened cattle plunging to their doom
Your neighbors pass unseen.
Is there no time to idle?
Is there no place for dreams?

As I stand in your wonderful cities
My heart thrills in my breast;
Thrills in answer to an age old beacon
Calling me back to the West.

Bonnie Merchant, 1945

While Bonnie was handling disasters throughout the country, a near disaster happened on the home front. Son Mike was thrown from a vehicle and sustained a severe head injury that left him in a vegetative state. Bonnie and Mike's wife Rose became his therapists and over the years have helped him return to a normal, useful life.

Bonnie not only cares for family members when the need arises but looks after friends and neighbors as well. When Vera Neal was living alone up Moon Gulch in her last years of independence, Bonnie drove that winding shelf road each morning at 6 A.M. on her way to work to give Vera her daily medication and deliver her mail, which she had picked up the day before at the Rollinsville post office. This would be a generous act for anyone, but for Bonnie, who suffers from acrophobia, any shelf road is of the devil's making. Driving it in winter ice and snow was a heart-pounding, white-knuckle job.

Son George IV served in the Vietnam War, and when he returned home he brought a Vietnamese bride. This young woman was so appreciative of Bonnie's attention to her that she wanted to take the name "Bonnie" for her American name. To distinguish the two, she was called "Little Bonnie." Little Bonnie had left her family behind, and many of her relatives wanted desperately to join her in the United States. George and Bonnie took a leap of faith and sponsored eleven of their new daughter-in-law's family members, some of the first Vietnamese refugees to enter this country.

One Sunday in the summer of 1975 Betty and I looked out the dining room window of the cabin to see a string of people walking up the road. They were Bonnie, George, Little Bonnie, and the eleven Vietnamese refugees. As they filed into the cabin one at a time, they each introduced themselves by their new American names. "I Tina," "I Carol," "I Helen," and on down the line. Little Bonnie translated as best she could, given the eruption of chatter, but what we lacked in verbal communication we made up for in smiles and hugs. Teenage Carol was coaxed into singing a Chinese song, a memorable climax to a heartwarming occasion.

Oldest and youngest of the 11-member Vietnamese refugee family sponsored by Bonnie and George Merchant. They are Hua Thien Phan "Tina," 2 1/2, and "Auntie," wearing a traditional Chinese outfit.

The number of family-connected members of this Vietnamese group has grown from eleven to 135. The first group started a small Vietnamese restaurant business in Denver, and through their cooperative efforts now own five thriving restaurants throughout the city.

After serving the Red Cross for forty-five years, Bonnie was offered early retirement at age sixty-two. The timing was right, as George had been diagnosed with incurable cancer of the spine, and Bonnie needed to be at home. His last wish was to travel to Seattle to visit son Pat, with whom he had some unfinished business. Against Bonnie's better judgment, she put George, his oxygen, and his wheelchair in their Subaru and started on what she calls the "trip to hell and back." It was a hard six days to Seattle, and the return trip of eleven long days was worse. There were times at the end of a day of travel that George said, "Just leave me here and go on. I can't make it any farther."

After an extremely difficult time for both patient and caregiver, George died in May, 1986. We had a memorial service at the Pioneer Cemetery, and his ashes were placed at the foot of a large quartz rock, close to the grave of his parents.

During her Red Cross years, Bonnie had worked with a big hunk of man, John Cashion. Sometimes she was his boss, and other times he was hers. They admired each other personally and professionally, and when both of their spouses were in their last stages of life, Bonnie and John were often on the phone consoling each other. They began to see the possibility for more than a friendship, but they continued to focus their attention on their mates until their deaths.

John lived in Durango, and Bonnie stayed on at Merchants' Claim, but they began spending time together whenever schedules and distance permitted. On November 22, 1991, they were married, and after a time John moved to Lump Gulch. While Bonnie had always been the giver in most relationships, she has now become a receiver. John cannot do enough for his Bonnie. She has to be careful what she looks at when they're shopping. She's apt to have a surprise gift when they return home.

There are many facets to Bonnie's life. She is interested in most anything you can mention, especially the history of the area she has chosen to call home. She is a member of the Gilpin County Historical Society, and after her retirement served as curator of the Society's several museums. As the only paid staff member, her jobs were numerous.

Because of her interest in Colorado history, Bonnie participates in such special days as Central City's Lou Bunch Day, making her own costumes and playing the parts of early-day women of the street. She and John are regular performers in the yearly Cemetery Crawl, an event that takes place at one of several cemeteries in the hills above Central City. Each year history enthusiasts research the lives of early settlers of the area, create authentic costumes, and present their stories in one of the graveyard settings on an appointed afternoon in September. The affair is open to the public and is one of the Gilpin Historical Society's most profitable fund-raisers.

Bonnie is a lover of nature. She has an interesting relationship with a bear named Broom. He came to her door when he was a cub, and she shooed him away by brushing him on the nose with a broom. He continues to come for visits, but a wave of the broom reminds him that he is not welcome at the hummingbird feeders. She has an experimental garden which she hopes will tell her whether the wildflowers would rather be tended or left to nature's whims. She has built a pond and water fountain in

At one of the Cemetery Crawls, John and Bonnie portrayed John Quincy Adams Rollins and his second wife. John Q. A. Rollins guided the Mormons across Boulder Pass in 1865. The pass, southwest of Rollinsville, is now known as Rollins Pass and the settlement which Rollins organized was christened Rollinsville.

her back yard and is growing water plants. The Cashions' back yard is a regular bird sanctuary, with a variety of feeders to entice any birds that might be in the area.

Bonnie is a decorator. She decorates the windows of her home with seasonal art work, clothes Boris the statue in attire appropriate to the weather, makes fancy birthday and anniversary cakes, and each month creates a new garment for her large stand-up doll Betsy, which belonged to her grandmother.

A few years ago the Cashions took on a new project. They purchased a cabin on the south fork of the Lump Gulch road and remodeled it for Bonnie's hobby house. I'm not sure how long Bonnie has been interested in doll collecting and restoration, but long enough to have a large collection of dolls of every size, shape, and description. Now she has turned her hobby into a business, Bonnie Blue Dolls, where she brings old dolls back to life and returns them to their owners complete with such researched information as age, manufacturer, type of material, and their approximate value. She has restored four dolls for our family.

Ol' Timer residents and friends can't imagine mountain summers without first Bonnie and George, and now Bonnie and John. They have been our rescuers and our companions in so many ways: calling us to the telephone at all hours of day or night before we had a phone installed in the cabin; inviting us to take showers as often as we wanted before we got our bathroom; preparing Hamilton's cabin for summer use; furnishing transportation when a car broke down; bringing us up-to-date on winter happenings; filling us in on the history of the area; keeping our extra keys handy for when we lock ourselves out of The Ol' Timer; sharing food and fun; and participating fully in sing-alongs. John has harmonicas in almost every key and knows how to make the most of their capabilities. Bonnie spreads them on a table in front of her and hands him the one he needs for the song that has been chosen. It's not unusual to see them making eyes at each other when they think no one is watching.

There! I've done the best I can in describing my friend Bonnie, but it still doesn't do the job. As I said at the beginning of this chapter, "She can't be described on paper." You have to know her, experience her big heart, hear her easy laugh, get swallowed up in one of her bear hugs, enjoy her hospitality.

'Tis "her thinking of others…" that makes me think of Bonnie.

THINKING OF BONNIE

For the Newells' 50th wedding anniversary celebration, Bonnie baked and decorated a fancy cake.

Bonnie dressed as a "Madam," or "Lady of the Street," for the 1989 Central City Lou Bunch Day. She made her own dress.

My childhood doll, Phyllis Eileen, was in disrepair until Bonnie restored her. Now she sits proudly on my Aunt Beulah's spool bed, color-coordinated with the beautiful quilt made by my sister-in-law, Nell.

Bonnie's husband, John Cashion, who became Lump Gulch Mayor after brother-in-law Robert was recalled, adds his harmonica-playing skills to our sing-alongs.

Vera Neal

"There's a car coming up the road," I said to Merla one day as we were working in the yard. "I wonder if we're getting company?"

"It's not a car," Merla responded. "It's a truck, and it's pulling in next door." A couple got out and went into our friend Jim Murray's house, and in a few minutes, Jim was bringing them over to meet us.

That was our introduction to Mike and Vera Neal. We learned that Vera was the younger sister of Jim's wife Annie, who had died in 1941. From the time Jim had moved from Denver back to Gilpin, Mike and Vera had visited him weekly. Every Saturday they'd come rattling up the Lump Gulch Road in their old black Dodge pickup to lend him a hand. Vera would do a little housecleaning, bundle up his laundry to take home to wash, and then the three of them would climb into the pickup and pop down to Rollinsville for groceries. We were told that, on rare occasions, Jim and Vera would stop off at the Stage Stop, the Rollinsville restaurant, bar, and dance hall, for a beer. Mike, a teetotaler, never joined them.

It didn't take us long to realize that Vera was no ordinary person, and as our friendship grew over the summers, we learned interesting things about her life and the way people lived in those hills during the mining days.

Though I wasn't recording stories at the time, I did take some notes, and these are things I remember.

Vera was born in Kewanee, Illinois, in 1888 and lived in Illinois until 1915, when Annie and Jim invited her to come to Gilpin and live with them. Vera accepted the offer to come to Colorado and took a train to Denver. From there she boarded the Moffat Special to Rollinsville, where the mail carrier met her and took her to Jim and Annie's home. The date was January 9, and the countryside was a wonderland of clinging snow. She remembered that the post office and general store were both in the same building across from the boarding house. The Tregays invited her to dinner at the homestead ranch the first Sunday she was in town. She was impressed with the square grand piano in their living room and was surprised to discover that the oldest son Tom could play it quite well. Grandma Tregay explained that Tom had taken piano lessons in Denver.

Sam Daugherty, Gilpin postmaster and merchant, Tom Gill, Jim Murray, Ann Murray, Vera Gill, in town of Gilpin, 1917

Dancing was a popular activity for young and old alike. Sometimes these get-togethers were held in the schoolhouse, and sometimes in people's homes. Jesse Williams was living at Snowcrest, later The Ol' Timer, the log cabin which he had built in the 1890's. He and his wife were separated at the time, and his wife Miranda and daughter Snow had moved to Boulder. Jesse liked young people and was always having dances and parties at Snowcrest. Jim Murray often played the violin at these affairs, and he and Annie both played guitar.

Gilpin schoolhouse in early 1900's

Tom Gill was the most likely bachelor in town, so the young people and Jesse decided to play matchmaker. They planned a party at Snowcrest and invited Vera and Tom, hoping the two would hit it off. In keeping with their plan, they asked Tom and Vera to go to the kitchen and make sandwiches. Vera's first impression was not favorable. She thought Tom was a big show-off. Tom's impression of Vera was quite different. He picked up on her fine qualities that first night. As Vera got better acquainted with this good-looking, fun-loving young man, her opinion changed. They began courting, and after two years of enjoying parties and dances together, he proposed and she accepted. They were married in 1917 and moved to their first Moon Gulch home, which was just over the hill from The Smuggler Mine, where Tom worked. Vera said the mill ran night and day, and if it stopped in the middle of the night, the quiet wakened them. In 1926 they moved to their second Moon Gulch home, which they named Mooncrest. This was to be Vera's home for the rest of her life.

Tom and Vera Gill at Smuggler

Bill Briscoe was a neighbor and close friend of Vera's, and he loved to recall stories she had told him. Bill had his own way with words, and since he had grown up in Mississippi, he had a Southern drawl that added a flavor to his storytelling. His eyes brightened as he spun his yarns, and he usually had a handkerchief or a napkin in his hand which he worried to death, twisting and turning it, while he talked. I can see his face and hear his voice as I write these stories as he told them to me:

> *Tom and Vera were great on dancing. I guess at that time they were not having dances in Rollinsville, so they went on a regular basis down to Golden some 25 miles away. She said that he'd get off work at the Smuggler Mine, and they'd hitch*

a horse up to the spring wagon and leave in the early afternoon. They'd get to Golden about nine o'clock, in time for the dance. They were so glad to be seeing people and having some fun, that they'd dance most of the night. She said they hardly ever got back home on Sunday until nine or ten in the morning. Sometimes they'd get caught in a snow storm and have to stay at one of the ranches along the way. One time they stayed over at the Rollins Ranch off highway 119. She said they had baked beaver tail for dinner. It's the only time she ever ate beaver, but it was considered quite a delicacy.

> *Let me tell you about the first car they bought. Tom didn't have the slightest idea about how to drive it, and nobody could tell him anything. They bought this car down in Boulder, and the salesman wanted to teach Tom how to drive it, but Tom said, "No, just open the door." So Vera got in with him and they started up Boulder Canyon. Well, you can imagine what Boulder Canyon used to be like, a steep, winding , rough dirt road, and Tom didn't know what to do about shifting gears. It'd stall and he'd get it started, and they'd chug along till they finally worked their way up to the Moon Gulch Road. You know how hilly and twisty that shelf road is, but there's that one place where it straightens out and is flat. Vera said when Tom got to that stretch of road, he hit the foot feed, and they tore along like it was a race track. She said, "We could get to going 25 miles an hour." Whenever I used to take Vera someplace, we never went across that stretch of road, no matter where I was taking her, that she didn't say, kinda to herself, "The race track road."*

Tom left his mining job in 1930 and went to work with the county road maintenance crew. One morning in 1941, Vera said goodbye as he went out the door to leave for work. Suddenly he turned around, came back into the house, grabbed her and said, "I forgot to kiss you." Vera had told me this story several times, but I'll tell it in Bill's words:

> *She knew when he left that he was going to be working over on South Beaver, but right around noon, I remember she said, she heard the grader coming up the road, you know. And from hearing it she knew it was him on it, and he came with the blade down like he was grading the road. She said he waved and she waved back, but he didn't stop at the house. He'd taken his lunch, but she thought maybe he'd decided to come home for lunch, but he just went right on up the road. Well, she kept waiting for him to come back, but he didn't come back. Somebody, whoever was maintenance supervisor, came up in a car sometime later and told her that he had died of a heart attack that morning over in Beaver. She said, "No he didn't. He just came by here not long ago and waved at me when he went by." She never gave up her belief that Tom's ghost had been driving that grader.*

Of course, I never knew Tom. He died twelve years before we bought the cabin, so for me, it had always been Vera and Mike. Vera had told me how she and Mike had met, but I asked Bill to review that story for me to be sure I had the details correct.

Bill complied:

> *Jim and Annie had moved to Denver, and when Annie died in September of that same year, Vera went to Denver to stay with Jim. She was no city gal, and she missed her mountains and her home. She came back to visit whenever she got a*

chance. On one such trip, she got off the train and stopped in at The Stage Stop in Rollinsville to say hello to her friend Mary Cotter. Mary said, "Well, how you gonna' get up home?" and Vera said, "I guess I'll walk." Mary said, "Well, here's Mr. Neal who has come up here to live and is working on the road now, and I'm sure he'd be glad to take you up to Mooncrest." Mike was more than happy to be of assistance, and as he and Vera bounced their way up the Moon Gulch Road, they discovered that they were enjoying each other's company. When they got to her place, Mike said, "Do you have anything to eat?" and she said, "Not much." "Well," said Mike, "We gotta do somethin' about that," so they went back to the store and bought whatever she needed for the immediate time. Mike would always chime in and say, "And we've been eatin' together ever since."

The new friendship blossomed into romance and some time later Mike went to Denver to propose. When he asked for Vera's hand in marriage, he said, "I know you can never love me the way you did Tom, but I'm a good man and I'll do every-thing in my power to be a good husband." They were married in September, 1942. Vera always said, "I couldn't have had two better marriages. I was so lucky."

One day when Florence Gooch and I were visiting Bill in his Denver home, where he spent his winters, Florence said, "Tell us again about the time Vera won the prize for writing a jingle." "Oh, yes, the Christmas dinner," Bill mused. "That's a good one."

Well, Tom was out of work at this time, and there was just no way to get any cash, you know. It was during the Depression and the mill had closed, and they were just hoping to find a way to get something to eat. The Denver Post had a contest. It was somebody to write a jingle about Purina or something. Well, Vera wrote a jingle and she sent it in and didn't hear anything from it. She remembered that the only thing they had in the house to eat just before Christmas was some dried beans, and that was going to be Christmas dinner. But in the mail on the day before Christmas, here came this check for $5.00 for winning the jingle contest. They took the check into Rollinsville and cashed it, and, of course, at that time you could buy a lot of things for $5.00. They bought a turkey and everything they could think of that would go with a Christmas dinner and spent the last dime. They invited all the bachelor miners in the gulch in for that dinner, and she said it was one of the best Christmases they ever had. Just after that things turned around, and Tom got a job, and it all worked out for them. The little jingle was just a four line couplet—she told me once what it was, but I can't remember.

Vera was a staunch Republican and an active supporter of party candidates, especially Dwight D. Eisenhower. However, she confided during one of my conversations with her, "I was Republican Chairwoman and Mike was Republican Chairman, and we always did all these things for the Repub-lican Party, but," she chuckled, "nobody knows it, but I didn't always vote the Republican ticket. I voted for whoever I thought was the best man."

Vera had a friend named Charlotte who lived in Eldora, not far from Nederland. They had many mutual interests, including their loyalty to the Republican Party. After Charlotte moved to Omaha, Nebraska, to take a job as commercial artist, she met and married Ray Bokowski, and the Neals and Bokowskis sometimes met in Denver at Republican Party meetings. Their friendship continued to grow, and Charlotte decided she'd like to honor Vera with a special gift. Eisenhower was President at the time, and she arranged to meet with him when he was staying at The Brown Palace in Denver. He agreed to let her make a portrait sketch of him, and after he autographed it, she gave it to Vera. The signed portrait hung in the living room at Mooncrest over Vera's desk. It was a good like- ness of Ike, with his round face, receding hairline, and engaging smile. Vera was very proud of it and often men-

To Mike & Vera Neal

Dear folks: Well, your autographed portrait of "IKE" is done and awaits you to pick it up at Mr. Hosakawa' Empire magazine editor of the Denver Post. He is up on third floor clear around to the left off the eleva- tor. I was in Denver last week end just long enough t make the sketch and met Ike. I am for him more than -ever. He remembered you clearly and talked of you. The picture is framed and I hope you can get a little good publicity for Ike by displaying it in a well- known place. Of course it is yours and yours alone. It was so hot when I was in Denver. I went on the train and could not get up to see you. Dick amd Rita will see you soon. Lots of good luck folks and believ you me I am pulling for IKE! Love Charlotte...& all. Tell dear Jim hello and tell Mike that I showed his snapshot to a gal in Denver who thought he was IKE!

from Charlotte Bokcouski

tioned how it had come into her possession. One day when I was visiting her and we were reviewing the story, Vera showed me a postcard and asked if I'd like to have it.

Vera had another good story involving her friend Charlotte. In 1953 Mike and Vera still had no

The photo of Mike and Vera sent to Strike it Rich *in 1953*

electricity at Mooncrest. Mike's job didn't pay very well, and they couldn't afford the cost of installation. There was a program on TV called *Strike it Rich.* People could send in their stories of a person or per- sons with some special need, and celebrities would volunteer to answer questions in order to raise the money required to meet the need. Charlotte, in her concern for Mike and Vera's primitive living condi- tions, sent a picture of the Neals and a story of their circumstances to the *Strike it Rich* program. She must have done it well, as Mike and Vera's story was se- lected. Helen Rose, a famous dress designer, was chosen to answer questions on Vera's behalf. The amount needed for an electric generator was $400. Helen missed one of the questions when she couldn't think of the word "pittance," so the amount received was $360. Charlotte took the money to the National Light and Pump Company in Denver and told her story. Again she was convincing, as attested to by the instal- lation bill, dated 10/31/53. It states, "One rebuilt Kohler Elec., as per special quotation, $360." Vera could never tell this story without getting emotional. She said that the first evening after the generator had been installed, when the lights went on in the kitchen, she went to the bedroom and cried.

KOHLER ELECTRIC PLANTS • GASOLINE ENGINES • DURO WATER SYSTEMS
SHASTA PUMPS • GARDNER - DENVER COMPRESSORS • PACIFIC PUMPS
HEATING   P & H ARC WELDERS   ELECTRICAL
EQUIPMENT   U. S. "V" BELTS & HOSE   APPLIANCES

National
LIGHT AND PUMP CO.
DISTRIBUTORS
1632 WAZEE ST. ★ TA.7700-AL.6855 ★ DENVER 2, COLO.

Customer's
Order No. _____   Date _10/21/53_____ 194___

M _____R. F. Bokowski (Charlotte)_____

Address _____2715 N. 47th Ave_____
_____Omaha_____

SOLD BY	CASH	C.O.D.	CHARGE	ON ACCT.	MDSE. RETD	PAID OUT	

QUANTITY	DESCRIPTION	PRICE	AMOUNT
1	Model 1A-1 Rebuilt Kohler Plt.		
	As per special Quotation	360 00	
	Via Truck		
	Paid		

ALL claims and returned goods MUST be accompanied by this bill

15644   Rec'd by

MOORE BUSINESS FORMS, INC., EMERYVILLE, CALIF.

Although Mike and Vera had the convenience of electricity after 1953, they never had indoor plumbing. They had a well with a hand pump outside the kitchen door, and an outhouse up the path. Vera was in her late 80's when Mike died at age 90. Bill Briscoe decided she should not be taking those winter trips to the outhouse, so he had a gas-burning toilet installed in a back room of her house. At first she thought this was an unnecessary luxury, but she was soon showing it off and singing its praises.

Vera had a big celebration on her 90th birthday. She was remembered by friends and relatives all over the country. She was as alert as ever, but she was losing ground physically. She stayed in her home as long as doctors would allow, but she finally had no choice but to move to a nursing home in Boulder. She never considered selling Mooncrest or renting it to anyone, nor did she ever think of disposing of any of her possessions. She was certain that she would return.

I was sharing The Ol' Timer with Betty Campbell at the time, and on our last visit with Vera in the nursing home, we made arrangements to take her to lunch. "What food would you most like to have for lunch?" we asked as we made our way to the car. Her reply was swift. "Let's go to McDonald's for a quarter pounder." As we ate, she chatted about the things she needed to do when she got back up the hill. When we took her back to the nursing home and said our farewells, she said, "Next summer you'll visit me at Mooncrest." You might say that's what we did. Although she died that winter, her memorial service was postponed till summer, her favorite time of year, when her flowers would be in bloom. The service was conducted in the garden which she had enjoyed sharing with guests, and Vera Gill Neal was much with us. There is some talk of tearing down the structure which is Mooncrest, and that makes me sad. But Mooncrest is not Vera. Vera is mine to keep, one of my "forever friends."

TEL.: OXford 7-3322   Producer - WALT FRAMER

S T R I K E   I T   R I C H
THE SHOW WITH A HEART
1150 Avenue of the Americas
New York 36, N. Y.

October 5, 1953

Dear Mrs. Bokowski:

We received your letter asking to STRIKE IT RICH, and have selected it as a possible entry in our Helping Hand Mailbag, whereby some person, by proxy, tries to STRIKE IT RICH for someone listening in.

If you would like to have someone help you in this way, in which case all winnings, if any, will be sent to you, please exercise carefully, the following procedure:....

1- Sign the enclosed release forms at once, and return in the self-enclosed envelope. In the event that the letter sent us, was not written by the Helping Hand Recipient, then both the writer of the letter and the recipient, each sign a release.

2- If you are a minor, have your parent or guardian sign the release.

3- Inform us whether the recipient receives aid from his or her Local Welfare Board.

4- Tell us over which TV and Radio station the recipient receives STRIKE IT RICH in his or her town. In the event the recipient does not have a TV or Radio set, give us the TV and Radio station over which STRIKE IT RICH is seen and heard in the recipient's town.

5- Include any additional information, clear photos and clippings which might help to illustrate your story.

6- All pictures, clippings, letters, etc., become the property of STRIKE IT RICH, and will not be returned. We, therefore, suggest that you send us duplicates.

7- Due to the tremendous volume of mail received by the Helping Hand Department, we cannot guarantee the use of your letter after a period of 90 days from the date of your release.

8- IMPORTANT: Have your clergyman, mayor, doctor, teacher, employer; someone in authority who has knowledge of your case, and can verify it, sign the "NOTICE OF VERIFICATION", and have him forward it to us as quickly as possible.

Please remember that we cannot guarantee the use of your letter, and that we reserve the right to edit it. Good luck! Keep watching and listening to STRIKE IT RICH, for your letter may pop out of our Helping Hand Mailbag at any time.

Sincerely,

STRIKE IT RICH
HELPING HAND DEPARTMENT

VERA NEAL

Vera in her home at Mooncrest, 1977

Vera at her desk at Mooncrest. She was proud to display photos of family and friends.

Mooncrest, shed and garage, right; house, left

Esther checking on Mooncrest after Vera was gone. Sally says, "Admit it—you were snooping!"

GATEWAY TO ADVENTURE

One fine Sunday in July, 1985, sister Marj, her husband Robert, friend Florence Gooch, and I took off in Toho The Terribly Terrific Toyota for an adventure into the high country. We drove up Gamble Gulch till we came to the Tip Top Mine, where we turned right and headed up the more traveled jeep trails, exploring new territory. The flowers were at their peak. Bright yellow golden banner was snuggling up to brilliant red and orange Indian paintbrush. Soft blue and purple columbine swayed in the breeze, and lupine and loco were in abundance. The views of the range were spectacular, capped with enough of the winter's snow to give them a regal appearance against a cloudless sky.

We traveled for several hours, taking a right turn here and a left road there, not keeping track of our route. It was getting late in the afternoon, and we were hoping that we were close to the familiar Apex road. If we reached it, we would be able to get home before dark. Otherwise, it was the great unknown. As we came over the crest of a hill, we were startled to see a sturdy-looking metal gate with an authoritative stop sign gleaming red and white in the late afternoon sun. I halted Toho and jumped out to have a look. The lock and chain were impressive. So was the road ahead. We began to plot a risky maneuver. The hillside to the left of the gate dropped steeply to a road below. That road joined the road we were on and would allow us to skirt the gate. Could Toho and the driver handle such a steep sand and gravel descent? The driver, being me, was apprehensive. While we were pondering this option, a handsome new Chevy Blazer appeared, coming up the road toward us. Mr. Blazer stopped his vehicle and began to assess the situation; then he and his wife dismounted and came toward us. We all stood leaning on opposite sides of the gate discussing our dilemma. We learned from them that the Apex road was a short distance down the road. They had just come from there. They wanted very much to be on the road we had just traveled, and we, on the other hand, wanted to be on their side of the gate heading toward Apex.

I made what to me seemed a reasonable offer. Why didn't we trade my 1967 Toyota Land Cruiser for their 1985 Blazer and each be on our way? We could meet at an appointed hour in Rollinsville and trade back to our legally-owned vehicles. The Blazer owner took one look at Toho with its peeling paint, drooping rear view mirrors, and sagging door and declined the offer. Instead, he took a heavy cable from his vehicle, tied it to the metal post that held the chain and lock, fastened the other end to his Blazer, revved up his motor, and began to back down the road. The metal post gave a groan and began a gentle bend at the waist. Now it was easy to slip the chain from the post and fling open the gate. Each driver drove to the opposite side. We fastened the gate the best we could, waved good-bye to each other, and quickly moved on in opposite directions. We told ourselves and each other that it was illegal to fence off public roads and that we had a perfect right, indeed a responsibility, to make those trails available to the public. Besides, it allowed us to make it home before dark.

A couple of weeks later I was on the Apex road with another group of adventurers, and we decided to check out the gate, coming to it from the opposite direction. This time the chain was fastened to a pole which could not have been budged with a bulldozer. Private road or public, these gate owners meant business! We turned around and headed back to Apex.

GATEWAY TO ADVENTURE

A locked gate on a public road? This calls for action.

Public road or not, these gate owners meant business!

HELP! WE'RE LOST

It was a breathtaking view of the sunset, with the trees silhouetted against the darkening sky.

Toho plowed through the good-sized water hole with much displacement of water.

HELP! WE'RE LOST

One of the best things about summers at our Colorado cabin, The Ol' Timer, is that people have time to play. Most of our mountain friends are either retired or have come to their cabins for a vacation, and it's not hard to get a group together any time you want to stir up some excitement.

One especially fine afternoon in the summer of 1989, I ran across my yard to Marj and Robert's cabin and said, "Let's eat an early dinner and go exploring some back roads." By five P.M. we had rounded up Florence Gooch, who is always game for adventure, and our fun friends, Lin and Nancy Vrana. The six of us piled into Toho, my four-wheel drive Land Cruiser, and took off up through Chapman's meadow, past the War Eagle Mine, and around the bend to the Upper Gold Dirt. We had never followed that road farther than the mine and decided it was time to see where it went. Up and up we climbed to the tip top of the mountain and down the other side. Our first challenge was a good-sized water hole in the middle of the road. Our only choices were to go through it or to turn back. Toho would not be discouraged, so all passengers dismounted and walked through the woods to the other side while Toho and I charged through the obstruction with much displacement of water and cheers and shouts of encouragement from the team members.

The new trail led us to our old familiar Gamble Gulch road where we proceeded upward again, this time through the ghost town of Perigo. We knew that there was a high road which, if we took it, would bring us out at Missouri Lakes and on to scenic Highway 119 where we could enjoy a smooth ride home. There was also a shortcut off this road, a treacherous four-wheel drive path with dips that tilted a vehicle to its capacity. It would eventually wind its way back to Gilpin and The Ol' Timer. I had driven this road once years before and had sworn I'd never do it again, but what the heck. It was probably improved by now. The adventuresome spirit prevailed, and as I shifted Toho into "granny" gear and started to crawl down through the trees, we commented on the beauty of the evening sky. We hadn't gone far till we came to a left fork, and sister Marj said, "Have you ever taken that road?" I hadn't, and after receiving a "yea" vote from the passengers, I took what I hoped would be a safer route home.

We stopped at the top of a ridge where we could stand and survey great distances beyond. It was a breathtaking view of the sunset, with the trees silhouetted against the darkening sky. I still recall the exhilaration I felt, and that I sensed in the others. It was what I call a "razor's edge" experience. A beauty beyond comprehension. We stood for some time, reluctant to let the moment pass, until it finally occurred to us that the trip back in the dark might be more adventure than we'd bargained for. The road down the mountain had so many choices. At each fork we'd take a vote, agree on a course, and continue into deeper and deeper forest.

The darker it became, the narrower the road. As driver and instigator of this adventure, I began to feel some apprehension. Florence's husband would be expecting her home soon. We might come to an obstacle in the road and have to turn back—a grueling thought. As the trail became a path, Robert and Lin got out with their flashlights and walked ahead, throwing aside rocks and stumps, guiding us around gully washes and under low-hanging tree branches. I became totally disoriented. For all I knew we might have made our way over to Moon Gulch and onto Jumbo Mountain, or we could be on the hills above Tolland. Robert had gone around the bend with his flashlight and returned to say that we were in big trouble. The road ahead had been blockaded with large boulders. "We're not going back," I said, "Let's take a look." We found that with team effort we could move the rocks enough to make a path for Toho. We continued our outward signs of high spirit and jovial camaraderie, but my arms and legs were shaking from effort and tension. My stomach was knotted. "Why do I do these things?" I asked myself. We passed the blockade, and Robert took the lead again. This time he returned with the news, "We have to turn back now, there's a locked gate ahead and I can see a light coming from a building." "Civilization!" we hollered. "People! Humanity!" I jumped from Toho, ran for the gate, and climbed over. Heading for the beam of light, I hollered, "Help! We're lost. Is anybody home?" A door opened, an outside light came on, and a voice said, "Who's there?" "We're from The Ol' Timer in Lump Gulch and we're lost. Can you tell us where we are?" "Sure," laughed the voice, "You're in Lump Gulch, about three blocks from home. How'd you get past our blockade?" "Betsy!" I exclaimed, my eyes and ears making the association. "Betsy Burnett! Are we on your property?" Husband Clyde ambled out of the cabin, the adventurers collected at the gate, and what an uproarious time we had. We tried to swear them to secrecy, but they'd have none of it. We promised that if they'd unlock the gate and let us through, we'd re-build their fortress the next day.

The old Gilpin road never looked so good. On the short ride back to the cabin we promised each other that one day soon we'd take that trip in broad daylight and try to figure out where we'd been. That was several years ago and we haven't done it yet. Maybe next year.

MOLLY BALL

I was leafing through a folder marked "keepsakes" the other day and came across something I had scribbled on a scrap of paper after one of my visits with Molly Ball. I hadn't saved it for its poetic value. My attempts at poetry haven't improved much since fourth grade and the Harold Haber masterpiece. I had kept it because it was an expression of the joy I felt at having a friend like Molly. It was also a reminder of an evening I spent enjoying her company in front of the fireplace in her cottage which overlooks Snowline Lake. On this particular evening a full moon was rising in the eastern sky, casting shadows across the meadow and turning the lake into shimmers of sparkling gold. I had written:

TO MY GOOD FRIEND, MOLLY BALL

Oh, Molly—
You are a Ball!!!!
At ninety-two you sparkle like the dew drops
hanging from pine needles reflecting the morning sun.
What is your secret?
Have the roses which you nurture with such care
passed their grace and glory on to you?
You share your joys as freely
as the roses give of their beauty and fragrance.
Thank you for sharing tonight with me.

Your appreciative friend,
Esther Rings

Molly spent her winters in a retirement community in Denver and much of each summer at her cottage up Lump Gulch. She was still driving her 1960 green four-door Nash up and down those mountain roads when she was ninety-five years old. She would often bring a carload of her Denver friends to the mountains to enjoy the cool, refreshing air and to admire the variety of wildflowers growing in the meadow in front of her cabin.

During a visit with her in 1984, when she was ninety-seven years old, I asked, and was given permission, to begin taping some of her stories. The tape recorder made her nervous at first. She would point to it and say, "Choke that thing off for a minute." But once she was caught up in her reminiscing, the stories flowed:

I was born Amalia Maeder in 1887 in a small town in Iowa. My parents had
both come from Switzerland. My father had just started a small cheese factory in
Monticello, Iowa, when he took pneumonia and died. I was just a baby, the young-
est of five children, and my mother was pregnant with the sixth. There was no way

to keep the family together, so we were sent to live with various friends and relatives. There was an elderly couple who lived next to us, and I was taken to live with them. Although I was not adopted by them, I assumed their name and first went to school as Millie Gould. I was a bright child and can remember reading the newspaper to this old couple before I ever started to school. I didn't understand much of what I read but could figure out most of the words. These kind folks had a married daughter, Mary Miller, and when the old man died, the daughter took me to her home in Independence, Iowa, and I became Mildred Miller.

I was expected to do my part around the house, and I was assigned a variety of kinds of chores, such as cleaning the kerosene lamp chimneys and scrubbing socks on the old washboard. I was an industrious child, and if I had to wash the darned dishes, I did a good job. If I didn't behave as was expected, "Aunt" Mary would pull my ear lobes. I'm sure my ears are much longer than God intended.

One of the reasons I tried to mind and do as I was told was that I believed in fairies. I was sure that if you were a right good child and did everything you were supposed to, there would appear a beam of light that you could walk on right out to the moon. At that time I was a Methodist. At one time or another, I've been darned near everything. That little Methodist church had a small balcony, and Santa would come down the chimney to the balcony, and somehow he'd get from there to the stage. I thought he must be walking one of those beams of light.

The Millers lived by a little creek surrounded by many trees, and oh, that seemed like a great forest. The little stream froze over in the winter, and we had little skates. The space for skating was about as big as this room, but we thought we were really doing something when we'd skate on that frozen creek.

There was a corn canning factory in that little town of Independence, and about the only thing a child could do to make a few pennies was to husk and shell corn. If you shelled a bushel of corn, you got all of five cents. You could make maybe twenty-five cents a day. Well, I went to work at the cannery. Some years there would be lots of worms, big long things, and we were supposed to be sure there were no worms in the basket where we put the freshly husked corn. I was particular and kept the worms out, but there were other youngsters around me that just put worms and all right in the baskets. When I was twelve years old and working at this cannery job, I was told that I was being sent to live with an aunt in Colorado. I was never told the reason for that decision. That's just how it was. When it was time for me to leave, the cannery owed me fifty or sixty cents. I went to the manager, a little snip of a girl I was, and said that I was going to Colorado, could I please have my money? People didn't travel much, and Colorado was a very long way off, so they thought I was making up a story, and they wouldn't give me my money. Fortunately, I had a friend who later collected for me and sent me my small fortune.

Molly's move was to Elizabeth, Colorado, where she lived with her real Aunt Mary, her mother's sister. At that time she took back her birth name, Amalia Maeder. The name Amalia evolved into Molly, and she kept the name Molly Maeder until she married. Molly remembers always loving music, or anything else that brought beauty into her life. She said, "No wonder I sought things of

110

beauty. You can't imagine how barren the country was. I knew a lot of church hymns, and a favorite pastime was to take off in my swing, pumping as high as I could go; then I'd belt out those songs. It must have been awful."

The Elizabeth school must have had only eight grades, as Molly's aunt took her to Manitou, Colorado, a short distance away, to go to high school. Molly stayed and worked in a boarding house, earning her room and board by making beds, peeling potatoes, waiting tables, and doing other hard work. The second year at Manitou High School, she lived with a family named Haygee in Colorado Springs. Her jobs there were to scrub floors, wash diapers, and help care for their two children. In order to get to school in Manitou, across the viaduct, she bought a bicycle for about five dollars and rode as fast as she could in order to get to school on time. Because she never wanted to leave her chores undone, she often arrived late to school. Her punishment for tardiness was to spend an hour after school sitting in the library learning poetry—hardly a punishment for Molly, as she loved poetry.

It was while I was in high school in Manitou that I met my future husband, Max Ball. We were just good friends then, but the thing I liked about him from the start was that he was nice to everybody. To supplement the meager Ball family income, Max had learned to train horses and was hired to guide tourists on burro trips to the top of Pikes Peak. Manitou was a thriving tourist town in the summer, but in the winter it settled back to a few churches and schools. The high school was so small that there were only four seniors in Max's graduating class. After graduation Max received a scholarship to the School of Mines in Golden, Colorado, and his mother took in washings for the men students in order for Max to go to school. Because he had learned to handle horses and because he was an honor student, he got a job with the geological survey, a small organization of men in Washington D.C. There were no cars available to these men, so they spent their summers surveying the wilds of Colorado and Wyoming on horseback. Max took care of the horses. Later, his job took him to Washington D.C. During this time Max and I corresponded occasionally.

One of Molly's close friends in high school was a Swedish girl, Esther Paarken. Esther's sister Signa was seamstress for the upscale department store, Daniels and Fisher.

I was to graduate in the spring of 1905, and I hadn't an idea what I would wear. I couldn't believe it when Esther's sister, this wonderful seamstress, Signa, offered to make my graduation dress. It was just beautiful, all hand-made with lace across the bosom. I fancy it was the nicest dress in the whole graduation ceremony.

Molly learned about college scholarships from some of her classmates, so she applied for one at Colorado University in Boulder. She wasn't chosen, but the girl who had been chosen accepted an offer at another school, and the scholarship was given to Molly. Molly said, "Do you know what they said to me when they presented it? 'Don't disgrace us!'"

Molly remembered that "C.U. was a small school of two or three thousand. When you walked across campus, the men still lifted their hats. The streets were not paved, so when you crossed those muddy intersections you lifted your skirts."

During the four years she was in school at Boulder, Molly lived with Dean and Mrs. Hellums of the College of Liberal Arts and became friends with many of the professors. When she graduated, the Hellums helped her get a job teaching Latin in Brighton, Colorado. Her pay was sixty dollars a month for nine months. The next teaching job was in Trinidad, Colorado, where she earned ninety dollars a month year round—"a big amount," according to Molly.

The Hellums had traveled a great deal in Europe, and Molly was fascinated with the stories of their adventures. She began saving her money and making plans to spend a summer in Europe. Women didn't travel alone in those days, so she found a couple of friends to take the trip with her. One was Mrs. Libby, the wife of a philosophy professor at C.U. Because she was English and had traveled all over Europe, she was a perfect tour guide. The other traveling companion was Mrs. Hellum's sister, Mrs. Whitely.

> *That trip was quite an undertaking. It took three or four days just to get to New York. We sailed on the* Montania, *which at that time was the fastest boat you could get. It took a week to get to Liverpool. In London we stayed in an old manor house which had been converted to a boarding house. We had been told there would be bathing facilities, but we didn't realize what that meant. Our rooms were on the third floor. There was cold water on that floor, but the maid had to bring the hot water in a pitcher from the first floor. We didn't think that was much of a bath.*

During this part of the interview Molly's daughter, Jean, who had been listening quietly, interjected:

> *"Mother, you told us about a courtship on board the ship. Was it on the way over, or the return?"*

> *"Well, Jean, I didn't know I'd told you any of this."*

Jean continued, "Mother was a rare beauty. I have some photographs of her at that time, and I've been told by people what a beauty she was."

> *"No, I was never good looking, Jean, but I did have intelligence. I could discuss many things."*

> *Anyway, I didn't think of this gentleman as a beau or anything, just somebody I liked. I was still wrapped up in education. While I was teaching in Trinidad, my attitude changed. Max Ball wrote me a note that he had to come out from Washington to do some coal work, and he'd like to see me as soon as time and circumstances would permit.*

Molly Maeder (Ball) around 1911.

> *I remember that long, white gloves were quite the fashion at the time, and I went out and bought a pair in preparation for the big occasion. Max came right away and took me to dinner. He came every night he was in Trinidad, which was about a week, and by the time he went back, we were engaged. Max went back to Washington, and I finished my teaching at Trinidad, and we were married in August, 1915. Another of the C.U. professor's wives, Mrs. Ketchum, gave us a lovely wedding.*

A young Max Ball.

August, 1915. Max and Molly's honeymoon carriage. Max had arranged for a team of horses and a buggy to take his bride over Rampart Range to Woodland Park.

Then there was the honeymoon. A friend had loaned us a car, a little Ford, and after a night in a hotel in Denver, we drove to Castle Rock, where Max had arranged for a team of horses and a buggy. That conveyance took us right up over the mountain to Palmer Lake and on to Woodland Park, a little mountain village. We spent our honeymoon in a little cottage there and roamed the Pike's Peak area. Then we were off to Washington D.C. by train— Max with his new bride.

Molly described Washington D.C. as a little country place with not many cars. She said that if you drove a few miles out of town you'd probably scatter a big group of chickens, or a dog would come barking at you. However, because World War I was in full swing, in many ways, D.C. was very much alive. A representative of the Royal Dutch Shell Company of Belgium visited Max and asked him to go to Wyoming to the salt creek fields to organize an oil company. The big war ships were beginning to burn oil instead of coal, so acquiring oil was important to the war effort. Max and Molly moved to Wyoming, hoping to settle in Casper, but it had become such a boom town that there was no place to live or have an office. Molly remembered that it was so crowded that working men shared rooms and beds in shifts. When one man went to work, another was waiting to take his bed. Since Casper was out of the question, the Balls located in Cheyenne. Apparently Max's job was still connected to the geological survey, as the men and women he worked with in Cheyenne were part of the survey crew.

While we were in Cheyenne, the Spanish influenza struck the country all at once. There were many quarantines put on people. Most of the young men and women of the geological survey were staying in a large boarding house, but Max and I had been invited to use a wonderful old two-story house. We rented the place for the winter, and it became the social center for the survey gang. They were only allowed to go from the boarding house to the office, and to our house.

Often when the survey boys would come to our home, they'd use our bedrooms and spend the night. In cleaning up, I'd find that they'd left a necktie or a shirt or a pair of glasses. I kept collecting these things until I had a basketful. Then I gave a party and auctioned off all this quality merchandise. People were buying back their own belongings, but we had a wonderful time, and the proceeds went to the Red Cross. That was the kind of fun we had. We made our own entertainment. We even put on Shakespeare plays. We'd assign everyone a part and then give them ten or fifteen minutes to hunt through the house for props and costumes. I tell you, the fun we had doing those things. We didn't lack for things to do during that terrible time.

We lost many friends in that influenza plague. We had a young geologist with a wife and baby. One night the wife became ill and was taken to the hospital. I remember cooking up chicken and taking it to the house but had to leave it on the porch. I wasn't allowed in. Then the young man had to go to the hospital, and both of those young people died. The grandparents came from California and took the baby. This fiber chair I'm sitting in is what they gave me when they were disposing of the young couple's belongings.

After the Royal Dutch Shell Company, for whom Max had been working, abandoned all its projects in the United States, Max organized the Argo Oil Company, and the Balls moved to Denver. Their son Doug had been born in Cheyenne in 1920, and daughter Jean made her appearance after they moved to Denver. The family loved the out-of-doors, and the Rocky Mountains begged for their attention.

After we moved to Denver, we started taking Sunday excursions into the mountains, taking our picnic lunch, hiking and exploring. We thought it would be lovely to have a little mountain hideout. At that time this property was part of the Tregay homestead. Tom and Gertrude Tregay were gone, but son Bill was here, and Myrtle, who had married a Nerheim. We had a windfall, maybe $500 or so, and with that we bought the land and built our mountain retreat. There was a carpenter in Lakewood who had hay fever and a garrulous wife, and he was delighted at the prospect of coming here and escaping both. He brought three carpenters, and in a day they put up our garage. They put in bunks, a chimney, and a stove, and that's where the carpenters lived for the summer.

Max had some friends, Mac and Linda McKinstry, whom he had met through church functions in D.C. before he and Molly were married. The McKinstrys had left Washington to homestead around Jackson's Hole, Wyoming, but had not found the area to their liking. Mac had decided that he'd like to raise silver fox and beaver, so he started looking in the Denver area for a place to start his new business. Max took Mac all over the Rocky Mountains looking for the ideal place. When they came to the Tregay land, with the stream running through it, Mac said, "This is it! We'll settle here." Max got interested in the venture, and the two men organized a company and started a silver fox farm.

Our carpenters built a cook house and the fox pens and the McKinstry cottage next door, and Max and Mac began business in earnest. The foxes were treated like we treated our children. Their meat was cooked, and all the utensils had to be scalded. There was much disease, and many foxes died, so they had to be very careful. The McKinstrys weren't actually the caretakers of the fox farm. There was a lovely young girl in Denver who was an artist. She married a man named Jim Childs, and the two of them came to look after the foxes. They stayed two or three years; then Jim developed Hodgkin's Disease which eventually took his life. There was a succession of caretakers after that. Things were going quite well. The silver foxes were a beautiful sight, and they were selling for a good price. Then the Depression of 1929 hit everybody. No one could afford to buy silver fox, or any other kind of luxury. The McKinstrys had no reserve money, so they moved into the ranch house, the old Tregay homestead, and Mac taught school in Gilpin or Rollinsville to keep the family going. He eventually found the altitude too high, so he sold the fox farm to a local man, Art Crow. We moved from Denver to Canada in 1936 but kept our cottage in the mountains. The McKinstrys moved to a lower altitude but kept their cottage, also.

From Canada the Balls moved back to Washington to help with the war effort. Max knew all the oil men, and the companies got together to form the oil and gas division of the Department of Interior during World War II. Max became the head of this government agency. Molly laughed when she told me, "The government paid Max and the other department heads a dollar a day." When the war was over, Max was asked to reorganize the oil and gas division for the Interior, and later he became a private consultant and traveled all over the world.

> *During this time Max built us an elegant home. It was in a wooded area near Georgetown, right across the Potomac. We had all kinds of trees: three kinds of oaks, plus dogwood and hickory. I loved digging in the dirt and created a beautiful garden with many azaleas. It was just a joy.*

> *Max had less than a year to enjoy our new home. He died of a heart attack in 1954. I stayed on for about fifteen years. In the meantime various family members and friends used the mountain cottage from time to time.*

In 1969, Molly's daughter Jean, who was living in Israel, came to help her move back to Denver. Molly did some fixing up of her mountain retreat, and from then until her death she enjoyed entertaining family and friends in her cozy cottage.

On a day in July, 1986, after we had interrupted one of our interviews long enough to walk in the meadow and admire her Mariposa lilies, Molly said, "Crank that thing on. I'm ready to give you some history of this area."

> *At the foot of our property there was a hotel back in the early days. I think the foundations were still there when we came here. There are a couple of mining properties on this place, the old Cardinal and the Grenell. Various people operated the War Eagle during the Depression. When McKinstrys were here, they screened off areas of the stream to trap beaver. They used chicken wire fence with strips of tin at the top. The beaver didn't dig under. I don't know why. I've seen deer leap over those fences, and it looked as though they never touched the ground. There were often deer around the house, too. One summer before we had the back porch screened in, there were bear tracks leading to the porch.*

I was anxious to record any bits of Gilpin history Molly could remember, but just as we were getting started, Jean mentioned that her mother looked tired, and we'd better stop for the day. I made an appointment for the following week, but just as I was packing my tape recorder to leave the cabin, the skies opened up and rain came down in sheets. We set another date, but Molly began having health problems, and her family took her back to Denver.

Before I left for Kansas and another year of teaching, I was able to talk with Molly on the phone. We agreed to continue our interviews the following summer.

That winter I received a postcard from Molly's daughter Jean. It was dated February 11, 1987. I still have the card but am choosing to copy the words so that they may be more easily read.

Dear Esther,

Thank you for Mother's Valentine. She died on Saturday, the 7th, after nine days of a bed-ridden ordeal in her own apartment. Doug, Caroline, and myself, with the help of the nursing staff, tended her. She was very tired, had lost much of her hearing and taste, and wanted to die. We had celebrated her one-hundredth birthday on December 10, and she felt she had lived too long. I suppose without a heart pacer her time would have been shorter. She was very brave, and also witty, and quoting poetry. An hour before she died she sang a Swiss song of her Mother's. Doug, during the days, would sing and play to her in the afternoon. When I told her she had been a beacon for those coming along after her, she said, "Well then, let us join a chorus of happy memories."

I am so grateful that you taped her stories! Her body has been cremated, and we plan to scatter the ashes on Saturday near Olive's Knoll. My son Ronnie will be present, as well as Doug and Caroline's children.

All the best to you,
Jean

Olive's Knoll is an outcropping of rock on a hillside between the Ball and Nerheim properties. It was named after Olive James, a science teacher at East Denver High School. Olive worked for Max in his office when the Ball family lived in Cheyenne, Wyoming. Later she moved to Denver. She had two silver foxes on Lookout Mountain, and when Max and Mac started the fox farm in Gilpin, she brought her foxes to their farm and became a partner in the corporation. She bought ten acres next to the Ball cabin, and when she died, she left it to the Balls. Molly's ashes were scattered among the ashes of her husband, Max, and those of a grandson, son of Doug and Caroline, who had been killed in an accident.

Olive's Knoll is within walking distance of The Ol' Timer. It's a fine place to picnic, or meditate, or to sit and survey the landscape, and pay tribute to a grand and gracious woman, my friend, Molly Ball.

Caroline Ball, Doug's wife, displaying her art work at a street fair in Blackhawk

Jean Ball, Max and Molly's daughter, also an artist

Doug Ball, Max and Molly's son

MOLLY BALL

Summer, 1979. Molly sitting in her fiber chair in the living room of her cottage.

Summer, 1980. Molly surveying her wildflower garden.

Molly's cottage, torn down in 2000.

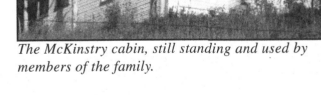

The McKinstry cabin, still standing and used by members of the family.

Molly's front meadow had a fine crop of Mariposa Lilies.

THE LOCAL 7/11

Jim Murray's little cabin next to The Ol' Timer had several owners after Jim died. For both sentimental and practical reasons we wanted it for our own. Jim's ashes were buried in the front yard, and we knew with certainty that his spirit dwelt within those cabin walls. That was the sentimental part. One of the practical reasons was that sister Marj and brother-in-law Robert wanted Jim's place for their retirement getaway. Another practical reason was that a recent owner had dug a well in the back yard. Although it was a shallow well, only twenty-five feet deep, it was considerably better than the one in our meadow with its rusty water and slow recovery.

By the time Marj and Robert retired in 1974, we had made a deal with Earl Hoffman to purchase Jim's cabin for $1700. Lump Gulch now claimed a number of year-round residents, and all of their mail boxes were lined up in front of Jim's house, now Marj and Robert's summer home. Robert, sometimes called Bob or Red, is a first class "people person." He can get "hung up by the tongue" more easily than anyone else in the family. When neighbors stopped for their mail, Robert would hasten out to greet them, lean on their open car window for a chat, and write any new news or information on the palm of his hand to preserve till he could transfer it to a file card. With people who were new to him, he asked for their name, the names of family members, their address and phone number, where they came from, and most importantly, "Do you play a musical instrument or sing?" We used to chide him, saying that it seemed that more and more neighbors were waiting till bedtime to come for their mail. The truth was that everyone enjoyed Marj and Robert, and they were the center of social life in our mountain community.

After Marj and Robert bought Jim's cabin, we made a few improvements. The three small rooms were joined by a short hallway. We partitioned off the end next to the outside wall and installed a chemical toilet. We furnished the place with treasures from yard sales and used furniture stores and created a warm and friendly living/dining area. It had a hide-a-bed sofa which got frequent use, an easy chair, a drop-leaf table with chairs, a wood-burning stove, and various smaller pieces of furniture. In the bedroom we managed to squeeze a double bed, dresser, portable clothes closet, and shelves. We furnished the small kitchen with all the equipment Marj needed for producing amazing meals for upwards of ten guests. Turkey dinners, crock pot stew, ham and sweet 'taters, chili and cornbread made their way from kitchen to dining table and TV trays. There was always room for one more at the Hamilton table.

Marj and Robert had been in the grocery business both in Holton and Topeka, Kansas, and the shelves in their cabin kitchen resembled their original Corner Cash Grocery. It was very handy for The Ol' Timer dwellers, who were often short of needed grocery supplies. Our frequent trips to the Hamilton larder caused us to nickname their cabin the Local 7/11.

After the family reunion at The Ol' Timer the last of June, 1987, sister June and brother-in-law Chic stayed on at the Jaffe's cabin up the road so they could join us in the annual Fourth of July celebration. There had been so much togetherness during the clan get-together that the three groups—June and Chic at the Jaffe's, Marj and Robert at their place, and Sally and I at The Ol' Timer—had eaten quite a few of our meals separately after the crowd left. Sally and I had let our larder dwindle, and by Tuesday we had an impressive grocery list. While we were doing our morning chores, June and Chic came by and said that Chic was going to Nederland soon; did we need any groceries? We said our list was too long, and we'd go a little later. June stayed at the cabin while Chic went to town, and we visited the morning away, forgetting that we, too, needed to go to the store. Since June and Chic would be leaving in a few days, I invited them to dinner and called to extend the invitation to Hamiltons as well. I thought I'd fix chicken on the outdoor fireplace.

After June left, I went to thaw the chicken in the freezer and saw that there wasn't enough for six people. Maybe we should change the menu. Marj had mentioned having a canned ham and some jalapeno cheese. We'd borrow that, use our own potatoes, mushroom soup, seasoning, etc, and make a casserole. We'd have green beans and a fruit salad. June had said she'd bring cake and ice cream. I put the potatoes on to parboil and Sally and I sat down to a late lunch. We were just finishing when Florence Gooch and her daughter Margaret arrived to walk up Ellsworth Gulch with us to see the columbine.

We had much to share with the Gooches, and the afternoon slipped away. We said our goodbyes and looked at our watches. The casserole needed to be in the oven NOW as we were going to eat early and go for a hike. Sally got to work putting all our projects away so that we could use the table, and I tackled the casserole. When I opened the cream of mushroom soup, I realized that it was a can we'd left at the cabin over the winter, and it had frozen. The texture was awful, but I had to use it. When I went to mix it with some milk, I remembered that at breakfast we had thought the milk was a little questionable. A quick check revealed that it hadn't curdled yet, so I decided it would do. No time for cutting real onion. I grabbed the dried flakes, more dry than usual after sitting unused for a number of years, dug out a handful, threw in some Mrs. Dash and a few other odd seasonings, cut up Hamilton's ham and Hamilton's cheese and stuck the mess in the oven. I asked Sally if she'd put two cans of green beans on to cook, and she came back from the pantry asking, "What beans?" "Oh, gosh," I said, "we must have used the last can. We'll have to borrow from our Local 7/11." Never mind that they'd already furnished the ham and the cheese. By the time the beans were cooking, it was time to make the fruit salad. Sally made the mistake of asking what I was going to use for fruit. A quick inventory yielded half a cantaloupe and a few sad grapes. This was embarrassing. How much could you expect dinner guests to bring? Not ready to face them in person, I went to the phone and rang the 7/11 number. By the time Marj answered, Sally and I were giggling so hard that every time I got to, "Have you got any f-f—," we would explode in laughter and I couldn't finish. The last straw was when Robert had to bring his own coffee. Well, we did furnish the potatoes and the lumpy mushroom soup and over-the-hill milk. Our guests said the food was delicious. I can't wait till they invite us for a meal.

THE LOCAL 7/11

When Sally and I arrived for the summer, the Local 7/11 was open for business.

The Hamiltons and their guests had to bring food from the Local 7/11 when they came to The Ol' Timer for meals. Pictured: June and Chapin (Chic) Newell, Wanda and Glen James, Marj and Robert.

Whenever we left in Toho for a high-country adventure, Hamiltons said farewell with hats over their hearts. They were sure they'd never see us again.

Neighbors stopping for mail in front of Hamilton's house got a warm welcome from Robert.

SUMMER 1984

There are many "predictables" at The Ol' Timer. As summer has followed summer over the past forty-eight years, we have joyed in the assurance that chipmunks and ground squirrels will beg at our doorstep, hummingbirds will flutter and sip at the feeder hanging outside the kitchen window, chicka-ree squirrel will eat peanut butter from a knife, summer guests will be many and varied, and songfests, jeep rides, hikes, picnics, and moon watches will make up a good part of the summer's entertainment.

Fortunately, each vacation also has some unique experiences. "1958? Oh, that was the summer that—." Summer 1984 had its share of memorable moments. There was the day that my good mountain buddy Florence Gooch and I decided to take a ride in Al Jaffe's rowboat on Snowline Lake. The lake is just up the road and around the corner from The Ol' Timer, a favorite destination for morning or evening strolls with guests. It is a lovely setting for viewing sunrises, sunsets, moonrises, and for watching a host of birds and animals. We exclaim at the sight of the great blue heron, red-winged blackbirds, and the noisy kingfisher. One evening two elk wandered into the area and had a bath at the edge of the lake, much to our delight. There are the mirrored reflections of Lindeman Peak to the south, the white-barked aspen trees to the east, and the quaint Jaffe cabin snuggled in among the trees to the west. My mind sometimes goes back to those ghost-town days when the lake was a peat bog, and the old Tregay homestead, turned fox farm, stood as a proud reminder of an earlier time. But I digress. Getting back to the boat ride: Snowline Lake is a fairly small, friendly body of water. Florence and I had life jackets, and though neither of us could swim, we hadn't the slightest concern that anything could go amiss. We "oh'ed and "ah'ed" over blue sky, fluffy clouds, jumping fish, and mama ducks transporting their babies on their backs. We rowed and chatted for some time, enjoying the sights and sounds and the feel of the sun on our backs. When we decided to return the boat to its resting place, I congratulated myself on my performance as skipper. I even brought the boat in at a pre-determined spot. Since there was no dock, no rope, or anything to hang on to, I thought I'd just jump ashore and pull the boat in after me. I made the mistake of stepping one foot onto the dry land first. At that very moment the boat chose to follow the wind and the waves and head back to the lake. This put me in a precarious position. One of my legs went north, the other south, and the rest of me hung suspended in between. In a desperate attempt to retrieve the disappearing appendage, I flipped over, landed in the water, and managed to separate myself from the boat. And there I sat. I don't remember how Florence and the boat made it to shore, but Florence is very bright and capable. She probably waded in, pulling the boat behind her. I kept telling Florence I'd be okay in a minute, but a sharp pain kept me from moving. My boating partner finally drove the half mile to the Hamilton cabin to get sister Marj, who was at her usual morning chore of whacking dandelions with an old-fashioned sickle. The two women returned with pain pills, towels, and a blanket and hoisted me out of the water and into the car.

This happened on a Friday, and it was Monday before a doctor was available at the local clinic. It also took me that long to locate a pair of crutches. So for two days I scooted around the cabin and yard on my seat. It was not fun. I cleaned a lot of dirt off the cabin's vintage 1954 linoleum flooring. Then there was the outhouse, that clever invention for homes without plumbing. Because of their pungent odors, they are usually placed some distance from the rear exit. The cabin outhouse is no exception; it is "up the hill." In order to keep my hands clean and my seat from wearing out, I'd place a small, thin pillow inside the rear of my jeans, put on an old pair of work gloves, and scoot my way through the house and out the back door. I'd back my way up the dirt path to the "Gilpin Annex," as our three-holer is called, up the steps, across the stoop, through the small door, and hoist my seat onto the outhouse seat. I didn't make any unnecessary trips.

On Monday the clinic doctor explained that I had torn the large hamstring muscle in my right leg. A neighbor loaned me crutches, and for a couple of weeks my activities were somewhat curtailed. But not much. Though the injured leg whined at any bearing of weight, it was soon willing to push the brake pedal on Toho, and away we went, a carload of us, up Gamble Gulch, and on to Tip Top Mine. I still chuckle when I remember how awkward and uncomfortable it was to squat, one leg bent and the other extended in front of me, when we all stopped in the woods for a bathroom break.

Back to the subject of "seats." I am reminded of another memorable day in the summer of 1984. I usually enjoy thunderstorms at the cabin. It's a good time to fire up the old Estate Oak in the living room, pop a crock full of buttered corn, and work on the bird puzzle, or the outhouse puzzle, or read, or nap, or do whatever strikes my fancy. But the storm on this particular day in August was not distant rumbling and gentle pitter patter. It roared and cracked at close range, and then the lights went out. Niece Sally and great-nephew Brian were spending part of the summer with me, and they had brought our adopted dog Whitey into the cabin because Whitey hated storms. As the situation intensified, we all collected in the front bedroom to protect each other. After thirty years of resisting such a modern convenience as a telephone in my "Ol' Timer" cabin, I had decided after the boating accident to have one installed and placed by my bed. The lightning saw this as a great opportunity. With a crackle and a flash, it tore through the telephone wire into the bedroom and jumped across the room to my seat. It happened so quickly, there was no time for high drama. It simply lifted me a couple of inches off the floor and back again. A brief inspection showed that I had fared better than the phone. It was dead. I was only tingling. I couldn't understand why the lightning had chosen that particular destination until later in the day when I was describing the incident to friend Florence, who had dropped by. "It got me right here," I said, and patted my right hip. I felt a bulge that wasn't me, and then it dawned on me. A full set of cabin keys in the hip pocket of my jeans had been responsible for this shocking experience.

Summer of '84? That was the summer of our adopted dog Whitey.

Dog Whitey was a wonderfully special dog. She had been named Freddie by her owners, and it was obvious that at one time she'd had good care and a loving home. During a family break-up her owners had neglected her, and she began to appear regularly at Marj and Robert's cabin next door. We all adopted her, and she became a great favorite of Sally and Brian. I liked Whitey just fine, recognizing her gentle, loyal nature and sharp intellect, but during all the years at the cabin I had fed and courted chipmunks and ground squirrels. I had never let dogs inside our fenced-in yard. Summer '84 was different. My authority was usurped. Whitey not only reclined on the kitchen stoop where the wildlife fed but was often sneaked into the back room during thunderstorms, or for a warm, comfortable night's sleep. Occasionally she made her way into the rest of the house. I think this was probably the first summer that I'd ever spent time alone in the cabin. Sally and Brian had gone off somewhere, and Hamiltons were visiting the Newells in Oregon. I was having trouble sleeping at night, partly because I wasn't accustomed to the solitude, and partly because we were having an unusual number of mice that summer. I'd lie awake listening to sounds I usually slept through, the scamper and chew coming from unwelcome varmints, and the creak and groan of those old cabin walls. In desperation I decided to let Whitey sleep in the front bedroom with me. What a comfort my watchdog was. I'd waken to mouse noises and say, "Wake up, Whitey. Sick 'em, Whitey." Whitey would open her eyes, sigh deeply, close her eyes and fade away. I'd lie with eyes wide open, staring at the ceiling, waiting for the next sound of mouse toenails clicking across the linoleum floor. Whitey only slept with me one other time. That was the night that a booming clap of thunder frightened her into a leap onto my bed. Well, not exactly onto my bed. She landed with uncanny accuracy right in the middle of my solar plexus. Whitey was a big dog, part collie, at least seventy-five pounds. That was a heap of leap.

Summer '84? That was the year that great-nephew Brian turned the back room, the bunkhouse, into his private electronic studio. I had always been grateful that, though the cabin wiring was old, somewhat dangerous, and with few outlets, at least the cabin was wired for electricity when we bought it. Now, with all of Brian's equipment, I began to consider the advantages of those old oil-burning lamps and coal-oil lanterns. The electric meter on the side of the house was whirring full speed most of the day, and often into the evening. The room was arranged something like this: Brian's television set claimed space on the dresser. On a stool in front of the dresser drawers, so that the drawers were not accessible, rested his computer. Brian could usually be found sitting on the bed with his boom box hooked to earphones which were hooked to his head. The rest of the room was a maze of wires, cords, antenna—from window, to TV, to computer, to boom box, to Brian. All of these electrical necessities had to be connected to one outlet, the light socket which hung from the ceiling.

I was just getting accustomed to the outer-space sounds escaping from that dark dungeon when nephew Dale arrived with his two boys, Steve, 11, and Mike, 12. Delighted as I was to see them, I had to stifle a strong impulse to leave home as I watched them unpack two electric guitars, an electric keyboard, an amplifier, and a boom box. All of this, plus a suitcase or two, was piled into Brian's studio which, in addition to his gear, already housed bunk beds, double bed, dresser, trunk, two stools, a bench, curtained closet area, and several storage boxes. I did many outdoor chores that week, and we all spent time hiking and exploring the back roads in Toho. Thanks to careful monitoring by parents, and an auntie rule or two, we managed the week with good grace and created many moments worth remembering. The three boys were full of ideas for dramas and musical performances, and the instruments were used to provide the adults with evenings of entertainment. I saved a copy of a printed program the boys made for one of their performances.

125

```
┌────────────────────────────────────────────────────────────────────┐
│                              OUR SHOW                                │
│       WELCOME TO THE BIGGER, BETTER, (Economy Sized) EDITION OF…     │
│               THE RINGS-KRUEGER-RINGS VARIETY SHOW                   │
│                                                                      │
│  THE PLAYERS: BRIAN KRUEGER, MIKE RINGS,   GRANNY… (an old lady who's got some- │
│  STEVEN RINGS                              thing coming to her)… Mike Rings    │
│                                                                      │
│  PART I                                    JOE HANNIGAN… (our hero)… Brian Krueger │
│                                                                      │
│  INTRODUCTION: BRIAN KRUEGER, STEVE RINGS  SNYDE MCLOW… (our villain)… Mike Rings │
│                                                                      │
│  AIN'T SHE SWEET (Our Version)             EVYLIN HAWKINS… (Granny's daughter)… │
│  (Don't Let This Fool You About the Rest   Steve Rings               │
│  of the Show)                                                        │
│                                                                      │
│  IT'S A HARD LIFE                          ACT I    THE BANK IN THE MIDDLE OF │
│  Brian Krueger, Mike Rings, Steve Rings              NOWHERE         │
│                                                                      │
│  BEATLE MEDLEY                             ACT II   SAME AS ACT I    │
│  (Arranged by Mike & Steve Rings)                                    │
│                                            ACT III  THE TRAIN TRACKS OUTSIDE OF │
│  HEY JUDE,                                           THE TOWN        │
│  MICHELLE                                  ACT IV   GRANNY'S HOUSE    │
│  (Sung by Brian Krueger)                                             │
│                                                                      │
│  BIG DUTCH                                 VICTORY SONG              │
│  Brian Krueger, Mike Rings, Steve Rings    Mike & Steve Rings        │
│                                                                      │
│  PART II                                   THE CASE OF THE ONION BURGER │
│                                            (A Mystery with M.C. Grannigan) │
│  INTRODUCTION:    (same as above)                                    │
│                                            MEDLEY FINALE             │
│  MELODRAMA                                 Mike & Steve Rings with Brian Krueger │
│  CAST (in order of appearance)                                       │
│                                                                      │
│  BANK TELLER… (also doubles as sheriff,        THANK YOU FOR YOUR ATTENTION │
│  judge, mailman, etc.)… Steve Rings                                  │
└────────────────────────────────────────────────────────────────────┘
```

The following winter I took a leave of absence from my Kansas teaching job to begin writing my cabin stories. I stayed with Sally, Brian, and David in Tempe, Arizona. When the three of them were at school, I had time for quiet meditation, reflection, contemplation, and planning. As I thought back over the events of that interesting summer, it occurred to me that I hadn't always been in charge. I resolved that next year I would be more assertive.

For Brian's September birthday I wrote the following parody to the song, "There is a Tavern In The Town."

I Have a Cabin in the Pines

Verse 1

I have a cabin in the pines (in the pines)
all covered over with hops vines (with hops vines),
and there I sit in quiet reverie
until my nephews come to me (come to me).
They bring computer and TV (and TV)
and amplifiers 2 or 3 (2 or 3).
With guitar and keyboard, ghetto blaster, too.
My quiet reverie is through (it is through).

Refrain

Fare thee well for I must leave thee.
Do not let my parting grieve thee,
but this generation gap has got me in its grip.
It's bleep and blast and twang and tweet (twang and tweet).
I know you think these sounds are neat (sounds are neat),
but my ears are raw, I've simply blown a fuse.
I'm going to take a summer cruise.

Verse 2

As if the noise were not enough (not enough),
I have to take that "doggie" guff (doggie guff).
Oh, it's "Whitey" this and "Whitey" that,
and "Whitey needs a loving pat" (loving pat).
But now I think how it would be (it would be)
to have a cabin just for me (just for me),
with no bleep or blat or twang or tweet.
It really wouldn't be so neat (be so neat).

Refrain

I've decided I won't leave thee,
I will live with you in Tempe,
And together we will bleep and blat and twang and tweet.
We'll celebrate each special day (special day)
in quite a ceremonious way (-' monious way).
So here's a toast to a kid who's really neat.
We hope you'll like your birthday treat (birthday treat).

The birthday treat was a color portable TV. If The Ol' Timer was going to be subjected to another summer of TV, why not color?

SUMMER *1984*

It's Jaffe's lake, and Jaffe's boat, and Florence (R), but she made a better choice of company on this trip.

Florence and I have shared summers of hiking, jeeping, and sing-alongs since 1969.

Mike, Steve, and Brian performing one of their melodramas.

Brian at the keyboard during one of the evening performances.

A guitar duo by Mike and Steve.

Whitey reclined on the kitchen stoop where the wildlife fed.

129

TALES OF THE FOURTH OF JULY ROAD

The Fourth of July road is one of our favorite summer ventures. It's an extension of the Eldora road which takes off from highway 119 at the south end of Nederland and follows Middle Boulder Creek through the town of Eldora. A few miles up the road from the town, a left fork leads to the old town site of Hessie, and a right fork, the Fourth of July Road, continues to Buckingham Campground and a number of high mountain trailheads. These include trails to Arapaho Peak, Arapaho Saddle, and Arapaho Glacier.

We discovered this challenging jeep road during our first cabin summer, 1954, when we were showing our "very own mountains" to family and friends. We didn't have a four-wheel drive at the time and chose not to take our cars past the town of Eldora because of the narrow, rocky, dirt road. However, a number of us did manage to hike another few miles to a beautiful double waterfall which we later learned was Helm Falls. Just below the falls we discovered a group of four well-kept cabins with intriguing shutters. Each shutter had a brightly colored painting. We could recognize a witch-like character on one shutter, and others had pictures which we thought might be telling stories of mining days.

We were curious about these cabins, wanting to know who owned them and what the pictures were about. Each year when we took the Fourth of July Road, we stopped to visit the mystery cabins and make up stories about the meaning behind those pictured shutters. The cabins never seemed to be inhabited, and we were about to claim them for our own when, in the summer of 1984, we chanced to meet a woman who was well acquainted with the cabins and their original owners.

By then we were the proud owners of Toho, our four-wheel-drive Toyota, and Marj, Robert, some guests, and I were bouncing down the narrow Fourth of July Road, returning from a hike. In front of us, we saw a line-up of cars facing both directions. Since they were not moving, I stopped, and Robert and I got out to locate the problem. We learned that a YMCA bus was stalled in the middle of the road and no one could pass. In the next hour while we waited for a tow truck we chatted with fellow motorists. A lady strolled by to check on the situation, and we engaged her in conversation. "I'm Ruth Buchan," she told us. "I have a summer cabin on the rock overlooking Helm Falls." I came to attention. "The green cabin with the screened-in front porch?" I asked. "Yes, that's the one," she replied. I couldn't believe my luck. "Do you know anything about the cabins below you? The ones with the brightly colored shutters?" She did. In fact, she had spent her honeymoon in one of them. Because I wanted to tape our conversation, and since I was eager to see her place, I asked for an interview.

A week later I charged up the Fourth of July road in my trusty steed, located the obscure driveway to Ruth Buchan's cabin, and knocked on her door. She greeted me warmly and invited me to join her on the screened-in porch overlooking the falls. The porch was more than a porch; it was also a bedroom. The hand-made bunk beds were constructed of lodgepole pine logs, still covered with bark. Through the doorway into the rest of the cabin was a dining area with table and chairs, a couple of easy chairs, and a partitioned kitchen area. A small wood cooking stove and a huge fireplace were the only sources of heat. All modern conveniences were purposely excluded. No electricity, no running water, no telephone. More rustic even than The Ol' Timer. I started the tape recorder and said, "Tell me about yourself and this neat old cabin." She began:

I met my husband in one of his classes in English literature at Washington University in St. Louis, where I went to college. After a proper courtship, we were married in 1933 and came to Colorado on our honeymoon. We stayed in one of the cabins just below Helm Falls. These cabins had been built the year before, in 1932, by the Robertsons and their daughter, Sheila Burlingame, and her husband. Sheila was an artist in St. Louis, and when she heard we were to be married, she said, "Use my cabin in Colorado for your honeymoon. I won't be using it this summer." The Burlingames had built their cabin next to her parents', intending to spend vacation time there with their son. However, Sheila's husband had died in Denver on the way home to St. Louis just after their cabin was finished. This summer, 1933, Sheila was going to go with an artist group to Cape Cod, and her parents, the Robertsons, had other plans also. We were given directions as to where to find the key and the cabin, and we made our way to that charming cottage, where we spent the summer. We were the first ones to stay in Sheila's cabin.

People complain about the road now, but you should have seen it then. It was so narrow there was nowhere to pass. If you missed a rock on one side, you were more than likely to hit your fender on one on the other side. As you can imagine, we fell in love with this valley. The second summer we rented another cabin close by and found the land we're sitting on while looking for a lost dog. Because it was not far from the waterfall, had a view of Arapaho, and overlooked the whole valley, we thought it was a great place for a cabin. After a bit of inquiry we discovered it was on Forest Service land. We went to the Forest Service and got a lease to use about half an acre and build a cabin. We pay a "use" fee for the land. At that time it was $5.00 a year. It's now $400. The cabin cost about $200, including furniture, and it costs me much more than that every year for the "use" fee and the taxes. The cabin is essentially as it was 50 years ago. We cook on our wood stove which Robertsons gave us the year we built, saying that although it had a crack in the front of it, we could use it until we could get something better. We carry water from the well in a bucket, light up the gasoline and kerosene lamps at night, and use the two-holer up the path. The three children and nine grandchildren say, "Please don't ever change anything. We love it just as it is."

When Ruth showed me the fireplace chimney, she told how her husband had hauled all the rocks for it on a rock sled. They built the cabin and the fireplace by themselves. Her husband had died fifteen years ago, and she had continued to spend each summer in her cabin on the rock, sometimes alone, but mostly in the company of family and friends. A tent in back handled the overflow of guests.

"More about the Robertsons," Ruth said after a little stretch and some refreshments.

They had been in the mountains for many years. Mr. Robertson was an employee of the Public Service Company of Colorado. He worked for some time in Leadville building dams, enforcing mine safety rules, and working with water supply. They had chosen this site by the fall not only for its beauty, but because Mr. Robertson's family owned the land. They also owned a gold mine up on the side of the hill. They called it the Denver Mine and were certain that it was going to make them a fortune. They found a rich vein and took the ore all the way to England to be assayed so there would be no word of it in the Nederland area. The assay report was amazingly good, but the vein ran out almost immediately. They were always sure they would mine again and strike it rich, but it never came to pass. The mine entrance is on the opposite hill from the cabins. You can still see the remains of the bunkhouses, the shaft house, and the old cook house.

There were two brothers in the Robertson family. Bill was the engineer from Leadville, the father of Sheila Burlingame and my neighbor in the cottage down the way. He was also supervisor in the building of Nederland's Barker Dam in 1912. His brother Art was a ne'er-do-well who lived in a little log cabin up the creek. He was sort of a nut about explosives and was always blowing up a stump or something. We could never understand any reason for it. He just seemed to like doing it. Things came to a head one day when Bill, his daughter, and his wife were alone in their cabin. Art came down roaring drunk and was going to shoot his brother in a feud over the mine. He had a gun, so they knew he meant business. Little old Mrs. Robertson put her husband in the closet with a mattress over his back. Then she went up to Art and grabbed him by the necktie, twisting it till he was choking. With that, daughter Sheila came up from behind and bopped him on the head with a hammer and knocked him out. Sheila ran up to get my husband, who went for the sheriff. They hauled Art away and he was never seen again. The Forest Service took his cabin down because disreputable types were staying in it.

Bill's wife was Poet Laureate of Colorado in 1953. Her first name was Clyde. Her father had eight girls and gave them all boys' names. Clyde was very small, and her curly hair was quite white by the time I knew her. She was very attractive. She wrote some books of mountain ballads, which are really charming. Two of them are entitled, "Fool's Gold" and "Yellow Witch" and are illustrated by her daughter Sheila. The paintings on the shutters of the cabins are also done by Sheila and illustrate these ballads. The cupboards inside the cabin are, or at least were, decorated in the same way.

The interview was over, but there was still casual talk. I noticed a couple of painted boards which looked like some of the old shutters I had admired all those years. I was correct. They had been given to Ruth by the new owners of the Robertson and Burlingame cabins. One was of the Yellow Witch, painted by Sheila, and the other was a caricature of a stubby little fellow who frequented a bar in Nederland. It was done by Sheila's son, in much the same style as his mother's paintings.

Before I left, I took pictures of the shutters and of Ruth's cabin perched atop the hill overlooking Helm Falls. Ruth gave me copies of a few of the ballads written by Clyde, the Poet Laureate, with accompanying illustrations by Sheila.

I said my "goodbye" and "thank you," and headed down the steep, narrow driveway. In my excitement I barely missed a huge rock. I thought "That rock is intruding upon this driveway." Then I decided it was probably the other way around. The driveway was no doubt intruding upon that time-less rock. I made a sharp left onto the Fourth of July road, waved goodbye to Helm Falls, and made my way down the bumpy, water-puddled road toward Eldora. Around the first turn I stopped the car to gaze at the valley below. Just ahead, an aspen hinted autumn's beginning. High against the rich, blue Colorado sky, the leaves of a single aspen branch danced in the breeze, a shimmering ballet in red and gold. I thought of a quote from a favorite book, *The Prize*, by Flavia Weedn: "To live is the game, and I've already won, because life, life itself is the prize."

FOOL'S GOLD

by Clyde Robertson

Men have lived, and men have died
Where the peaks are glorified,

Never knowing that they trod
On the Golden Hills of God;

Never knowing stone and tree
Symbolize Divinity.

Eyes with money-narrowed lids
Never see the pyramids.

Sun glint on a canyon wall,
Aspen-glow and waterfall

Are but trifles to a man
Chasing colors in a pan.

All of life and all of hope—
Sand, beneath a microscope.

TALE AND SHALE

by Clyde Robertson

Up where peaks
Are wild and high
Winds are weighted
With the cry
Of men long dead:
The cry for gold, Ancient as
The world is old.

Eagles whet
Their hungry bills
Above a waste
Of wart-scarred hills;
Warts of tale
And shale that speak
Louder than
The tallest peak.

This, the end
Of man's mad quest—
Gray dumps where
The woodchucks nest.

Clyde Robertson (1870-1954) was Poet Laureate of Colorado in 1953. These ballads can be found in **Poney Nelson and Other Western Ballads** by Clyde Robertson, Carnegie Branch Library for Local History, Boulder, Colorado, Collection 777-1-1.

THE YELLOW WITCH OF CARIBOU

Mountain Ballad by Clyde Robertson. Illustration by her daughter Sheila Burlingame. Both were residents of The Fourth of July Road.

*"The yellow witch hides in these hills
And gets our men against their wills."*

*The hills are high in Caribou—
The air is clear—the skies are blue;
But where a black ledge seams the ground
The yellow witch's tracks are found;
And men grow drunk with ravishment
Once they have caught the witch's scent.
The aspens on the mountain side
Were green when Carlo brought his bride,
The cherry-cheeked Selina, to
The haunted hills of Caribou.
"You better take your man and go,"
The old wives warned, "before the snow.
The yellow witch hides in these hills
And gets our men against their wills."
Selina shook her bold, black head.
"My Carlo will not leave my bed;
He's signed up with the sawmill crew,
He's safe enough in Caribou.*

*"Who minds the talk of wrinkled crones,
Their skin a-stickin' to their bones?
Their men-folks might go trailin' round
A-chasin' witch tracks in the ground;
But my man's mine! I'm not afraid
I'll lose him to a stealin' jade."
"Child, we were all the same as you,
When we were brought to Caribou.
We know, as only old wives can,*

*The curse of havin' half a man.
We know the end of these old tracks—
The blinded eyes—and broken backs."
But when the mountain side grew red
And pulsing as a wanton's bed
Young Carlo's eyes flamed with the fire
Of an unhallowed, mad desire.
Selina knew his passion meant
"Her man" had caught the witch's scent.
Before the first snow veiled the crest
Like lace upon a woman's breast
She saw him leave the sheltering mills
To roam among the siren hills.*

*But no man yet has come to know
Which way the yellow witch may go;
She burrows deep in porphyry rocks
And bars her trail with granite blocks.
So Carlo did as all men do
That chase the witch of Caribou.*

*At last upon a sloping crest,
As rounded as a woman's breast,
Beneath a snow of winding lace
He tracked her to her hiding place.
Here, in an evil, blackened niche,
He mated with the yellow witch.
At dawn Selina found him there
Strangled, by a golden hair.*

135

POSTSCRIPT

When Ruth told me about using a rock sled to haul the rocks for their fireplace, I had never heard of a rock sled. But one day in late August of that same year, I was driving with my friend Howard Knoll up the road to the War Eagle Mine when he said, "Stop! I see something interesting." It was an old rock sled. It looked like a crudely built snow sled with wooden runners. Howard said they were sometimes called "go devils" or "stone boats." We hauled the rock sled home and had it in the yard for years. It finally fell apart. I should have given it to the Central City museum.

TALES OF THE FOURTH OF JULY ROAD

Ruth Buchan's cabin overlooking Helm Falls.

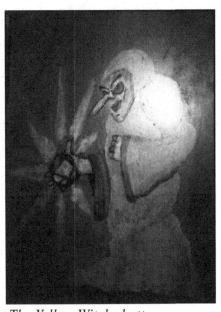

*The Yellow Witch shutter,
illustrated by Sheila Burlingame.*

*Esther sitting on the rock sled, sometimes called
a "go devil," or "stone boat."*

Esther photographing Helm Falls.

GRANNY ETHYL

"Childhood is life's first gift.
Whatever your age,
acknowledge your child within."
from *Play Therapy* by Michael Joseph

To give this story a proper beginning, I must whisk you off to Tempe, Arizona, for an explanation of how Granny Ethyl got her name. This story began in 1984, the year I took a leave of absence from my teaching job in Emporia and lived in Tempe with Sally and the boys. I was attending a Methodist church there and attempting to make myself known. You know I can't stand not having friends. When I was asked to light the candle of joy during the Advent season, I jumped at the chance. This would help people to know me and speak to me instead of looking the other way. However, the church bulletin for that day gave my name as Esther Wings, and when the minister introduced me, he called me Ethyl Rings. Sally and the boys and I thought it was pretty funny, so I wrote a story about it, and some of my friends got to calling me Ethyl Wings, especially Ken and Irene Shaw, my good friends from college days.

Now we can go back to The Ol' Timer, and I invite you to take another look at the color photos at the end of the chapter, "In Defense of Outhouses." In the chamber pot picture I am wearing a lovely pink robe which had been my cabin housecoat, actually outhousecoat, for upwards of twenty-five years. It met my needs so perfectly that I chose to ignore suggestions from family and friends that its time was past.

During Ken and Irene's cabin visit in 1992, they stole my precious robe and gave me a new one. College friends Jack and Doris Sutton were visiting at the same time, and the four of them created a lovely ceremony in which they hung my old robe on the crossbar of the gateposts leading to the cabin and celebrated its retirement with songs and eulogies. I was not impressed. In fact, I was in mourning.

The following summer the Shaws arrived at the cabin on the day that Sally and I were to attend the opera in Central City. Irene went with us, leaving Ken and the Shaws' son Jim at The Ol' Timer. When we walked into the cabin after our cultural experience, I was startled to see a life-size, homemade doll sitting in the wicker rocker wearing my beloved pink robe. The robe was carefully sewn to the doll's body. No easy on and off. This was my introduction to Granny Ethyl Wings, or Granny Ethyl for short.

That summer Granny was all over the place. We might find her in the outhouse or trying to drive Toho or playing the organ. She cheated when we played games and complained when asked to do housework. She became a cabin attraction, and when Larry McGrath's sister Linda Wiggs saw her, she was so taken with Granny that Jane and Larry decided to make a life-sized doll for Linda.

When Linda arrived at her Nederland cabin, called Colozona Inn, in the summer of 1998, Jim Davis was there to greet her, complete with a letter of introduction. Jim got his name from a McGrath family joke: In the days before private gates, fences, and "No Trespassing" signs, the McGraths—mother Zoe, father Dean, and children Linda and Larry—used to explore Colorado's back roads, sometimes ending up on someone's private property. If anyone were to question them about trespassing, Dean was prepared to ask, "We're looking for Jim Davis. Does he live around here?"

Jim and Granny became friends and often joined in cabin activities. They spent time together in the summer, sent cards, wrote letters to each other, and somehow managed to be together during the cold winter months. A romance developed.

When Granny wrote to Jim, she waxed eloquent.

June 11, 2000

Deer Hunnie Bunn,

I am goos bumps frum hed to toh ovur my ingagment braselet. It cum in thu male frum Ezirona. Whut a clevur way tu suprise me. Whin I seen thu pakage I nevur dreemed it wuz frum yoo. Yu must hav had it sent by ponee expres as it wuz stamped weeks ago and I nevur got it til yesturday. All them jems musta cost yu a hunk a that gold yu bin savin frum yur minin daze. Gosh, gee, yu shudn't hav dun it. It sur makes me sad tu tell yu thet its probly gonna be a loooooooooong engagmunt. I wuz so hopin we cud get hiched this summur, but it dont seem likly, dew to them skinflints thet pretend tu hav my best inturest at hart. Git this!! They rote me thet they gest cudn't aford a weddin this summur dew to thu fakt thet thu nu watur closet is costin so much. Now whie thu hek did they need thet nu concrapshun aniways. Hoo wunts to set indoars a medutatin whin yu cud bee injoyin thu fresh air and seenery? Besides, thu nu faciluty has jest won hole. I gess thay'll hav tu draw straws tu see hoo gets first tern. I hope thay dont tare down thet kute house out bak, cuz thets where I excape when thers wurk tu bee dun. Besides, I'm afeered the suctun on thet nufangled seet mite pull me rite down the hole.

Them skunks got anuthur reesun they kent hav a weddin this summur. They say there goin tu hav so many partees to inichiate there nu john thet there wuddn't be no time fur us to git hitched. Can yu beleve thet? Thay need tu git ther priorties strate.

I no yur not aloan nou and I wont be fur long, so its gonna be trikey to hav time aloan togather. Thu Hamulton cabun is gonna bee emptee so mabee yoo cen slip up sum nites.

Well, hunny bun, we'll dew thu best we cen. Meentime ill be warin my ingagment braselut evry our uv thu daee. I wunt fokes to no im took.

Loooooooooooooooooooooooooooooooooooooove.
Granny E.

Granny and Jim started making eyes at each other at this sing-along. Floor sitters: Jane McGrath, Linda Wiggs, Rich Wiggs, Esther. Couch sitters: Larry McGrath, niece Carol Gebhart, Jim amd Granny, Robert, Marj. Standing: Irene Shaw, niece Jan Pearson

When Jim wrote to Granny, he used only a few, carefully chosen words.

**Any time, any place...
but only you.**

**yur friend
Jim Davis**

In the summer of 2001, Sally and I were invited to Colozona Inn for a surprise party. We were to bring Granny. We knew it was to be some fine affair, though we didn't know what. Granny had already graduated from the robe to a square dance outfit, but this occasion seemed to call for a more stylish attire. We found the perfect "get-up" at Bare Necessities, a used clothing store in Nederland.

The minute we arrived at Colozona Inn, Granny was swept away from us. In a few minutes a trumpet fanfare sounded, a curtain was opened, and there sat the little family: Granny, Jim, and their new twins, Julia and Abbott. We were relieved to learn that Jim and Granny had slipped off and tied the knot, and that the twins had been created by a delightful neighbor of the Wiggs/McGraths, Julia Abbott. Julia's life is a fascinating story,

Sally: "We're overwhelmed! We didn't even know Jim and Granny were married!"
Esther: "They're just darling!"

but I must limit myself to a few comments at this time. She is 90 years young and practices the art of zestful living. She became fascinated with the stories of Jim and Granny and decided they should have children. Years ago her sister had begun to crochet two small dolls but had never finished them. Julia was inspired to complete the project and surprise the Wiggs/McGrath clan with them. She got the whole old-town Nederland Pine Grove neighborhood involved: Young Savannah Ames gave clothing for the babies and folks wrote poems and notes of congratulation, which Julia compiled into a "baby book." When Jane, Larry, Linda, and Rich hosted a Pine Grove picnic, the surprise was presented, and Jim and Granny took on the role of parenthood.

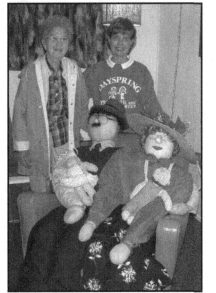

Julia Abbott created the twins for Linda Wiggs and Jim and Granny. Don't Jim and Granny look proud?

Granny Ethyl takes up a lot of room at The Ol' Timer. I sometimes threaten to have her meet an untimely end. I can picture a grand memorial service in the side yard of The Ol' Timer. There'd be balloons and bubbles, songs and stories. People would come from miles around, dressed in their new finery purchased at Bare Necessities, to celebrate a life well lived. But Granny is needed. She and her family have become a part of the mountain lore. Pretty inexpensive fun for quite a few people. Granny and Jim, Julia and Abbott are tucked away for their long winter's nap, but who knows what adventures await them, and us, when they reappear next summer.

GRANNY ETHYL

I was not impressed with the ceremony for retiring my robe. It had been my outhousecoat for 25 years.

Our new guest was Granny Ethyl. She was wearing my pink robe.

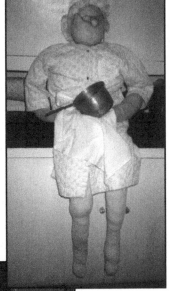

If Granny had to dry dishes, she sat on the counter. She said she had "very close" veins and couldn't stand for long.

When Jim Davis came into Granny's life, she got herself a square dance outfit.

Sometimes Granny escaped doing chores by sitting in the outhouse reading the Vitality magazine.

Julia Abbott, adopted grandmother of the twins, thought Jim and Granny looked great in their wedding finery.

WATER WAYS

"Ho, every one that thirsts, come to the water..."
The Book of Isaiah

Next week Dosia Carlson and I will be facilitating a journal writing workshop in Kirksville, Missouri. The women of the Methodist church in that city have chosen the theme, "The Waters of Life," using various water images as metaphors for the ebb and flow of life events. While my mind is swimming with the subject of water, it seems a good time to write my review of the sources and uses of water during the 48 years I've been at The Ol' Timer.

I mentioned in earlier chapters that our neighbor and friend Jim Murray let us use his boxed-up spring for our water supply the first few years of cabin life. It was our only water source, and since we dipped it from the spring and carried it in buckets through the aspen grove to the cabin, it was used sparingly. Even so, with the number of people we invited to be our guests those first summers, the water-way path was well worn. Those buckets of water were used for drinking, cooking, hand washing, dishwashing, spit baths, floor scrubbing, and laundry. You can imagine that cleanliness didn't hold the same importance that it does today. I'll describe some of the washing routines.

The Ol' Timer kitchen in 1954. The drinking water bucket sits on the counter by the stove. Note also the white wash pan on the Buck's Range, the vitreous wash bowl inching off the picture to the right of the sink, the tea kettle on the electric stove, and a variety of pots and pans.

Hand washing before meals: This took some coordination and a number of washing stations. We did have a kitchen sink which, at first, drained out onto the ground. That was one washing station. We also had an outdoor facility. A wooden windbreak had been built on the northeast side of the kitchen stoop. Its original purpose was to keep snow from drifting around the kitchen entrance, a practical feature for those early year-round residents of the mining days. Our male guests found a different use for it. They built a crude bench in front of the windbreak and hung a broken mirror, which they framed with log slabs, on the north side of the windbreak. Under the mirror they placed nails for holding wash pan and towels. This became their hand washing/shaving station. Other wash basins were kept in the back storeroom and on the dressers in the two bedrooms. It was important to keep the large blue enamel kettle filled and heating on the stove at all times.

The men in the family turned the windbreak by the kitchen stoop into their washing/shaving station.

Spit baths: Finding privacy for spit baths with fifteen or so overnight guests was another challenge. The men put hook and eye locks on the inside doors of the storeroom, but since it also served as the pantry, one's bath might be interrupted with such requests as, "Could you hand me a can of beans?" Sister Marj described spit baths in this way: "You take a thimble full of water, a wash cloth, and some soap. You wash down as far as possible, then up as far as possible, and then you wash possible." Niece Sally says that description comes from *I Know Why The Caged Bird Sings* by Maya Angelou.

Tub baths: This was definitely a once-a-week operation, and most guests left without the pleasure of this experience. But for those of us who were left behind, the instructions went something like this:

» Bring in wood from the woodshed and build a good fire in the kitchen stove.

» Take several trips to the spring and fill a couple of large pans with water for heating on the Buck's Range.

» Fill the teakettles and the blue enamel pot and heat them on the electric stove.

» Save some cold water for adjusting the temperature of the bath water.

» Put rugs on the floor in front of the stove and bring in the galvanized tub from its hanging place on the back side of the cabin.

» Collect towel, washcloth, soap, and clean clothes.

» Pour hot and cold water into the tub, getting the temperature just right.

» Strip, and hang clothes on the back of a kitchen chair.

» Fold your body, yoga fashion, into the tub of water.

» Have a friend standing by to replenish hot water and keep the fire going.

» Relax, and if it's daytime, watch the hummingbirds maneuver in and out of the feeding stations hanging by the kitchen window. If it's night, pull the shades.

» When your time is up, dry, dress, and begin emptying the bath water into the sink, dipping it out with a long-handled pan, one pan full at a time.

At this point it is essential to have a helpful second party.

» Helpful second party needs to be available to tip one end of the tub up as the water level recedes so that the water will collect at one end.

» When no more can be scraped from the bottom of the tub, you need the second party to help carry the tub into the yard and dump the dregs.

» Be sure to give the tub a good rinsing, as it will no doubt be very dirty.

» Hang the tub on the back wall of the cabin where you found it.

» Go back to the kitchen and mop up the spills, put the rugs away, and make things nice and tidy.

» By now you are hot, tired, sweaty, and need another bath, which you're not going to get for another week.

Laundry day: One of the large items which we toted from Kansas to Colorado in our first truckload of belongings was an old Maytag wringer washer. Young people who read this will probably not know how this machine worked. Some of the instructions are the same as for bathing, especially about getting the fire going and the water hot. One galvanized bathtub was not enough for laundry day. We needed two rinse waters, so we purchased an oblong tub to keep the round one company. On wash day the store room/spit-bath room, which was not very large, became the laundry room. Here are the instructions:

146

» Pull the Maytag washer out from the wall and place it a little east of center.

» Get the lime-green stool, which was a chair until it lost its back, put it next to the wringer side of the washing machine, and place the round tub on it.

» Get the old swivel piano bench with the split in the seat and put it and the oblong tub next to the lime-green stool in such a way that when the machine wringer swings to the side, the clothes will fall into the oblong tub.

» Now it's time to fill the tubs. You need a lot of hot water for three tubs.

» Make the washing machine tub water the hottest and the second rinse water in the oblong tub the coolest.

» Sort the clothes, sort of.

» Put soap in the wash water and a little blue bleach in the first rinse water.

» Dump a load of clothes into the machine and plug the cord into the one and only socket, which is on the north wall.

» The machine will begin to cough and groan, and then the agitator will start its back-and-forth motion—wishy washy, wishy, washy.

» After the machine has done its cleansing thing for about ten minutes, get the silky-smooth pine laundry stick from the corner by the back door.

» Use the pine stick to lift the clothes out of the hot water and put them to the lips of the wringer.

» If you have remembered to pull the lever that activates the wringer, you'll find that the clothes will go through the wringer into the first tub, and the hot water will flow back into the machine.

» Stir the clothes around until some of the soap is removed, and then swivel the wringer to the right (second position) and send the clothes through the wringer to the second tub, loosening more soap from the clothes into the second rinse water.

» Now swivel the wringer to the right again (third position) and wring the clothes into a laundry basket.

» String the clothesline from the kitchen corner of the cabin, to the leaning pine tree out back, and on over to the hook on the side of the leaning outhouse.

» Put a couple of poles (notched on top for the line to fit into) under the clothesline to hold it up so the wet clothes won't make the line sag.

» Take a clean cloth and run it along the clothesline to remove any dirt.

» Take the laundry basket of clothes into the back yard to let the sun and wind dry them.

On rainy wash-days Sally's boys, David and Brian, draped the wet laundry around the cabin.

» Hang the clothes neatly and in proper sequence: all socks together, etc.

» If it starts to rain, take the clothes in and drape them around the house; then start another load of laundry.

If the weather should happen to cooperate and your clothes dry on the line, you will find that the fresh-air smell of those garments, sheets, and towels as you fold them will make all this work worthwhile.

How did I get started on all of these recipes for clean living at the cabin? My original intent was to give a history of our water sources over time. I will now continue with my original plan.

In several of the chapters in this book I have mentioned the names of our friends Galen and Ula Ewing. Galen was county health inspector for Barton County, Kansas, and when he and Ula visited the cabin that first year, 1954, he took a dim view of our drinking water source. He suggested that, since Jim's spring water had not been tested for purity, we should add drops of Clorox into each bucketful of drinking water. We tried this, but as you can imagine, it ruined the taste of that delicious spring water. After company left, Merla and I went back to the original method of "drinking it straight."

Early in the summer of 1955, we learned that there was a community well in Rollinsville. It had a hand pump, and it was available to the public.

We collected gallon jugs, purchased a big funnel, and began getting our drinking water whenever we went to Rollinsville for the mail or groceries. Getting water from the well was a two-person job, with one person holding the funnel to the mouth of the jug and the other person pumping. We continued to use Jim's spring water for all of our other water needs.

I don't remember if the community well went dry or what happened that we couldn't use it anymore, but for a short time we got our drinking water from Kelly-Dahl Campground off highway 119 between Rollinsville and Nederland.

In 1955 Ray and Glayde Lezotte bought the Rollinsville Grocery Store from Slaughenhoupt and Slaughenhoupt (pronounced Sloggenhop), and once we had become friends with the Lezottes, we began getting much of our drinking water from a faucet at the back of their store. If we were heading in the direction of Central City, we'd stop at Cold Springs Campground off highway 119 and collect spring water from a metal pipe. The campground was rightly named; that water was deliciously cold.

Charles and Doris Sheetz of Topeka were good friends of Marj and Robert, and each summer for five or six years they joined the Hamiltons at the cabin for part of their vacation. Charles was great at helping with cabin projects, and it must have been the summer of 1958 that he got tired of hauling water and decided we needed our own well. He offered to contribute $200 toward this end, and we had a well dug in the aspen grove just west of the cabin. Neither Merla nor I had money to contribute to the digging of this well. The driller came with his big cumbersome equipment, and the cabin crowd gathered to watch, hoping to see water come shooting out of the ground. We told the driller, "When you get to $200 worth of digging, please stop." He did hit water at about 40 feet. It was never good, clear water, but it served for purposes other than drinking. We had hauled a hand pump from Kansas in a U-Haul, and for several years we hand-pumped all but our drinking water and hauled it from well to cabin.

Our first major upgrade was in 1965 when we purchased an electric pump. It sat on a platform over the well and had a pipe with a foot valve running down into the water. Another pipe ran across the ground to the cabin, through the cabin wall to a very crude faucet at the kitchen sink. On sunny days we had hot running water, and on cold days we had cold running water.

Summer, 1982. The hand pump had been put back on the old well in the aspen grove, and nephew Dale's boys, Mike and Steve, joined David and Brian in priming and pumping.

Marj and Robert got title to Jim Murray's cabin next to The Ol' Timer in 1976, and that property had a 25 foot well in the back yard. We put our electric pump on their well and had water piped to both cabins. Again, the plastic pipes were on top of the ground, with the same hot and cold feature, and we still got our drinking water from other sources.

When Golden Gate State Park was developed, it included a new campground, Reverend's Ridge. This became our drinking water source for a number of years. We'd put about twenty one-gallon containers and a couple of five gallon thermos jugs into the back of Toho along with three or four hardy souls in the Toho seats, and away we'd go. We'd drive our dirt road to Highway 119, head southeast to the Gap Road turn-off, take a left on that dirt road to the Reverend's Ridge turn-off, turn left to the campground and zigzag through the campground to our favorite water faucet. We got pretty fast at filling the jugs and carrying them back to Toho, especially if it was cold or rainy. We some-times treated ourselves to a little side trip before returning home. Just a ways on up the Gap Road, the Forest Service had built a lookout, Panorama Point, and the view it offered of the Continental Divide was spectacular. One early evening when we stopped to view the snowy peaks and admire a crimson sunset, we were treated to the gentle sounds of guitar and voice, a young man sitting on the overlook platform serenading his lady fair. I framed that moment and tucked it into my memory bank.

Before this choice spot became Panorama Point, our family and guests had enjoyed exploring three abandoned cabins that were perched on its highest point. One of the cabins was still furnished, and when the government demolished the structures, we rescued a small ladder-back chair which now sits by the old wind-up phonograph in the cabin living room.

Before Panorama Point was built, three abandoned cabins claimed the site. It was a great place to explore.

During the summer of 1988, seven of my friends from college days at Emporia State Teacher's College, Emporia, Kansas, joined me at the cabin for a reunion. The happenings of that week could be a whole chapter, but the gathering takes its place in the water chapter because in the middle of that week the Hamilton well ran dry at the same time that the rains began to fall. Fortunately, someone remembered a trick the pioneers used for accessing rain water. We put our tubs under the drain spouts, collected the water, strained it to remove the shingle dandruff, boiled the water to purify it, and used it for the most essential items.

The well recovered for a time, but by 1994 it was obvious that a new well would have to be dug. This time we were determined that the supply would be plentiful and that it would be safe for drink-ing. Because of the government land, the outhouse, and the swampy aspen grove, there was no place on The Ol' Timer property for a legally-dug well. The driller chose a spot behind the Hamilton cabin. In fact, he said it was the only spot on the two properties where he could legally drill. A huge drilling machine was brought in, and the crew struck water, four gallons a minute, at 400 feet and a cost of $8,000.

We hired a backhoe operator to dig a six-foot trench between the well and the cabin, but when the machine got within about six feet of the cabin, it hit bedrock. The operator said he'd have to blast. Ken and Irene Shaw and another college chum, Catherine Brown, had come for a visit just after the well digging. Ken heard the mention of blasting and said, "A blast that close to the cabin could knock out windows and loosen chinking." We had just spent $4000 to have a professional chinker redo most of the patch jobs we'd done over the years, so we weren't about to take a chance. Therefore, we chose to have the last piece of water line laid above freeze level on top of the bedrock. This meant that we'd have to drain the pipes in the fall before the temperatures plummeted, but since we don't use the cabin in the winter, this was a satisfactory solution. Friend Ken installed a pressure tank in the back storeroom, and by summer's end we had a good supply of cold, drinkable water coming through our funny faucet into our old chipped porcelain sink. This was a definite improvement.

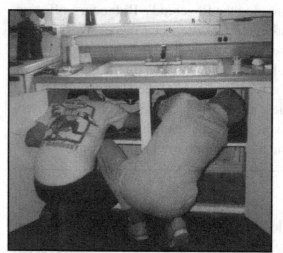

Larry McGrath and Ken Shaw spent many frustrating hours on the new sink, counter top, hot water project.

One thing calls for another when one starts any kind of upgrading. By the next summer, 1995, our abundant water supply had gone to our heads. We decided we might as well have hot and cold running water at our kitchen sink. This called for a new double sink, new faucets, new counter top, and of course, a hot water heater to sit in the storeroom beside the pressure tank. Through the years Ken Shaw has served as one of the cabin's maintenance men. He was on hand again to mastermind this project. Nederland friend Larry McGrath also volunteered his services. He hauled the water heater, sink, and counter top up from Boulder in his truck, and he and Ken spent long and frustrating hours installing our new water system.

The day that the hot and cold water came gushing out of the new faucets into the new double sink, which was cradled in the new counter top, called for ceremony and celebration. The working crew and a number of guests gathered in the kitchen and dining areas to hear the stories of "water ways" at The Ol' Timer, much the same stories that I have recorded in this chapter.

Various sentimental treasures were displayed: the old bucket that we used for hauling water from Jim's spring, the dipper and tin cup, the large containers for heating water on the stove, and a couple of clorox and milk jugs which had been used for water carrying through the years. Granny Ethyl was invited to share in the festivities, taking a place of honor on the new counter top. We were embarrassed to discover that she had "been in her cups" all afternoon, and she slumped, slumbered, and snored through much of the celebration.

I'm feeling water logged, and I'm sure you are also, but bear with me, there is a little more to be told.

When Sally came to spend summers at the cabin, spit baths and weekly galvanized-tub baths didn't meet her requirements. Our circle of mountain friends had expanded over the years, and a number of these families had indoor plumbing. We discovered that if we sat really close to them at sing-

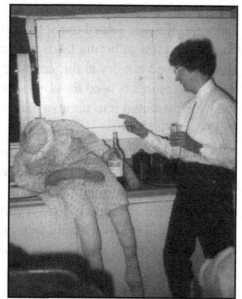

Granny Ethyl embarrassed us by nipping during the celebration.

150

alongs and other indoor affairs, we often got invited to "come over and take a shower." We accepted all invitations, but we knew that we needed our own facility. With the help of family, guests, and a neighbor contractor, Mark Van Everen, we drew up a plan for turning the back storeroom/pantry/spit-bath room into a real, honest-to-goodness bathroom, complete with shower stall, lavatory, and stool. Work began on the renovation in the fall of 1999, and by the time we arrived at the cabin in June, 2000, the interior work was completed. We managed to coordinate the back yard hole digging and the holding tank delivering within a few days of each other, and on June 29, 2000, The Ol' Timer cabin experienced its first flush.

We don't take this modern facility for granted. We comment on its convenience over and over, especially at night and on cold, rainy days. We are aware that some of the uniqueness of The Ol' Timer has been lost, but we're still close enough to our "water ways" to have a great deal of respect for them. Sam Keen, in his book *Hymns to an Unknown God*, says, "…we are ecologically immoral if we do not know where the water comes from when we turn on the faucet and where it goes when we flush the toilet." We know that our well depends on the summer rains and the winter snows, and we're aware that our 1500 gallon holding tank fills with amazing speed. This knowing helps us to treat with care and appreciation this "sparkling, glistening, whooshing, surging, trickling, life-giving WATER." (adapted from *Water Dance* by Thomas Locker)

WATER WAYS

When the boys got unmanagable, we hung them on the clothesline.

David liked bathing in the galvanized tub. Brian didn't.

1988 college reunion at the cabin. Front row: Irene Shaw, Margaret Herl, Rowean Nelson, Doris Sutton Back row: Ken Shaw, Jack Sutton, Esther, Orval Nelson

In 1994 the well drillers took over the Hamilton yard.

153

WATER WAYS

We had just had professional log chinker, Greg Weltzien, re-chink the cabin. "Please, no blasting near The Ol' Timer!"

Larry and Ken were making good progress with the sink, counter-top project.

The hundred-year-old Gilpin Annex looked forlorn framed by the huge backhoe which was covering the new holding tank.

June 29, 2000.
The Ol' Timer's first flush!

FULLENWIDERS AND OTHER FRIENDLY FOLKS

"Be grateful, truly grateful, for those good friends or thoughtful people."
Shawna Corley

I still miss the Gilpin County dump. For the first twenty years of cabin summers it was one of the social centers of the area. Located in the woods off the Lump Gulch road, it was a convenient side-trip as we headed to Rollinsville or Nederland for mail and groceries. It was more than a dump, really; we called it the Gilpin Exchange. If you thought that any of your trash might be someone else's treasure, you parked it on the bank at the edge of the dump abyss where it could be easily examined and rescued. Then you looked to see if there was anything you might need. Many dump treasures served useful purposes at The Ol' Timer for a number of years, and a few are still in use today. The spice rack in the kitchen, the oak wall shelf and mirror in the back bedroom, and the beautiful handles on the washstand in the dining room are a few of the items still in use.

We usually saved dump-doing until we could spare half an hour or so to browse. It was a busy place, and it was easy to strike up a conversation with the many customers. If you didn't want to talk about the weather or that gorgeous view of snow-capped Arapaho, you could always talk about trash.

It was while visiting the dump that we met Marie Rich, an artist who later did a watercolor of The Ol' Timer. And there was that wonderful, leathery outdoor woman, Martha Kimmering, who invited us over to see her place. She had a one-room cabin which she used for sleeping and for in-clement weather, but mostly she lived outdoors. She cooked her meals on the outdoor fireplace and had chairs and a cot out among the trees.

Indeed, the Gilpin Dump was an interesting and culturally enriching place, and it was a huge loss to us when they closed it in the mid-70's. Where were we going to find another multi-purpose social center? Sister Marj and brother-in-law Robert just happened to stumble onto a satisfactory substitute. It was the Nederland laundromat. It all started when Marj and Robert were making use of the facility one summer evening. Robert had taken his fiddle with him and was tuning up, and Marj was sitting with her feet propped against the dryer door to keep it from jiggling open, when in came a nice-looking couple who struck up a conversation. They were Lin and Nancy Vrana, newly married and quite smitten with each other. It didn't take Robert long to learn that they had a home on a hill above Nederland, that Nancy was musical, and that the couple shared the same kind of corny humor as the rest of our mountain friends. Besides being crazy, they were talented. Nancy was, and is, a ballet dancer and instructor, a pianist, and a com-poser. Lin is an artist, a writer, and a very capable handyman. He is

"Nancy the Ballet Dancer" is a painting by June Rings Newell, copied from a photograph.

also a duct tape specialist; he can mend anything from a broken chair to a torn jacket with a strip of duct tape. We began sharing social events, and the Vranas finally got up their nerve to introduce us to Nancy's folks, Jake and Edith Fullenwider. We've often pondered why it was that shortly after the Fullenwiders met us they went out and bought Lin and Nancy a new washing machine and dryer. Did it have anything to do with the kind of people they took up with at the laundromat?

Jake and Edith have a cabin on the Tolland road west of Rollinsville. Actually, it's not a cabin, it's a complex— four log buildings of various sizes, each with a special name and a special use. The Big Nut Hut is the Fullenwider's summer home, the Little Nut Hut is the guest house, and the Putt Putt Hut is the washroom. It gets its name from the motor that goes putt-putt as it draws water from the stream to the shower and lavatory. The Out Hut is a nice, clean two-holer nestled among the pines.

One of the Fullenwider huts

In 1983 Lin and Nancy invited me to spend an evening and night with them at the Fullenwider's cabin. After we'd shared stories around the fireplace, I took my leave and headed for a hot shower and a night in the guest house. As I stood in the moonlight with towel and toothbrush in hand, I had to think carefully about what I was to do in which of those quaint little huts. The thought of getting mixed up in my huts struck my funny bone, and the following night, in my own bed, my mind conjured up the song, "The Fullenwider's Cabin In The Pines."

Fullenwider's Cabin in the Pines
written in 1983 by Esther Rings

Verses 1 & 2
Down a winding lane, by a mountain stream
Stands the Fullenwider's cabin in the pines.
There are huts galore, not just two or three, but four.
At the Fullenwider's cabin in the pines.
There's the Big Nut Hut where the Fullenwiders dwell,
And the Little Nut Hut for their guests.
There's the Putt Putt Hut where you wash and brush your teeth,
And the Out Hut where you do the rest.

Chorus
Oh, it's Nut Hut here, and it's Putt Hut there,
And it's Putt Hut, Nut Hut, Out Hut everywhere.
And you stand there all confused
 wondering what the heck to use,
At the Fullenwider's cabin in the pines.

Verse 3
On a lovely summer's day I arrived there for a stay,
At the Fullenwider's cabin in the pines.
I got mixed up in my huts and I thought that I'd go nuts,
At the Fullenwider's cabin in the pines.

Interlude
Well, I brushed my teeth in the Out Hut,
And I slept in the tub in the Putt Hut.
In the Nut Hut I got dressed, and I'll let you guess the rest.
But the poor old place will never be the same.

Chorus
Oh, it's Nut Hut here, and it's Putt Hut there,
And it's Putt Hut, Nut Hut, Out Hut everywhere.
And I stood there in my skin,
Wondering where the heck I'd been,
At the Fullenwider's cabin in the pines.

Verse 4
If I ever go again down that winding lane,
To the Fullenwider's cabin in the pines,
I will write upon each door, numbers one, two, three, and four,
At the Fullenwider's cabin in the pines.

Interlude
Number one is where you eat with the family,
Number two is where you wash and brush your teeth,
Number three is where you sleep,
Number four—I'll say no more,
'Bout the Fullenwider's cabin in the pines.

Chorus
Oh, it's Nut Hut here, and it's Putt Hut there,
And it's Putt Hut, Nut Hut, Out Hut everywhere,
and I stood there as before,
wondering— one, two, three, or four,
At the Fullenwider's cabin in the pines

Fullenwider's Cabin in the Pines
written in 1983 by Esther Rings

verses 1 Down a wind- ing lane, by a moun-tain stream

Stands the Fu- llen- wi- der's ca- bin in the pines.

There are huts ga- lore, not just two or three, but four.

At the Fu- llen- wi- der's ca- bin in the pines.

verse 2 There's the Big Nut Hut where the Fu- llen- wi- ders dwell,

And the Lit- tle Nut Hut for their guests.

There's the Putt Putt Hut where you wash and brush your teeth,

And the Out Hut where you do the rest.

159

Chorus
Oh, it's Nut Hut here, and it's Putt Hut there,

And it's Putt Hut, Nut Hut, Out Hut ev- ery- where.

And you stand there all con- fused won- d'ring what the heck to use,

At the Fu- llen- wi- der's cabin in the pines.

Interlude
Well, I brushed my teeth in the Out Hut,

And I slept in the tub in the Putt Hut.

In the Nut Hut I got dressed, and I'll let you guess the rest.

But the poor old place will ne- ver be the same.

More about the Fullenwiders. Edith will celebrate her 92ⁿᵈ birthday in May, and Jake is following close behind. They had their 68th wedding anniversary celebration in December, 2001. The first anniversary I remember sharing with them was their fiftieth,when they invited a group of us from the mountains to join them at their ranch near Kiowa, Colorado, for an overnighter. Their spacious guest-friendly ranch house is at the edge of the Black Forest, where Ponderosa pines grow in abundance, bluebirds dart in and out of the birdhouses Jake has made, and deer wander through the yard at dawn and dusk. We had sing-alongs and nature walks, gift giving and story telling, and we broke bread together in a number of settings. The most memorable moments were on Sunday morning when we had our church service in the woods. We sang hymns and had a short sermon, but words weren't really necessary in that setting. Nature said it all.

We joined Jake and Edith at their ranch house to celebrate their 50th wedding anniversary.

We had our church service in the woods.

Jake and Edith are small of stature, but mighty of character, talent, and brain power. I wouldn't take anything for the hikes we've taken together, sharing favorite high mountain trails to Blue Lake in the Indian Peaks, and Heart and Crater Lakes high above Moffat Tunnel. They're not hiking so much now, but until a few years ago, whenever we headed for the high country, Jake and Edith led the pack.

Jake and Edith leading the pack on a hike to the top— the Continental Divide.

There are so many friendly folks whom I'd like to include in these pages. "Friendly Folks" could be a book of its own, but for now I must settle for a few brief tributes.

Merrill Slater was a bachelor who, along with Horace and Jo Price, owned the cabin up the hill north of The Ol' Timer. It had been built by Jonathan Williams, brother of Jesse, who built our cabin. We became friends the year of our cabin fix-up and were in each other's summer homes for meals, song-fests, and camaraderie. Slater, as he encouraged us to call him, became a favorite of Ol' Timer visitors, both family and friends. He was an interesting mix of country gentleman and rugged mountain man. Gourmet cooking was one of his talents, and on very special occasions his table groaned with mouth-watering food served on fine china. We sometimes visited him when he was working on his own cabin improvements, and he was a perfectionist in all he did. His neat chinking jobs put us to shame, and though we tried to master his technique, we never came close.

Like our friend Jim, Slater was a gift-bearer. He came down the path from his cabin one day looking quite pleased with himself. He had found a couple of whiskey flasks in the likeness of gold miners. The gold pans the miners were holding in front of them had the words "Old Timer" written on them. These tokens of friendship, though not exactly works of art, still reside in the glass-front bookcase in the cabin living room. Sally threatens to have them evicted, but I'll have none of it.

After one of our candlelight sing-alongs, Slater noticed that we were extinguishing the candles with our fingers. After his next trip to town, he appeared with a candle snuffer. He said, "No self-respecting dwelling should be without one." We still use it at the end of any candlelight ceremony, and it is a special reminder of one evening when he was simply bursting with song. He loved singing the old gospel hymns, and his deep voice filled every corner of the cabin. We had company at the time and had planned an "early to bed, early to rise" schedule, but Slater had a different idea. He kept calling out the names of one hymn after another until around midnight, when we were all hoarse and bleary-eyed, all but Slater.

Merrill Slater, country gentleman and rugged mountain man.

Merrill usually went down to Fort Morgan to be with his friends, the Prices, when temperatures dipped below freezing, but one year he spent the entire winter at his mountain retreat. That spring we received one of his letters with a pressed Pasque flower enclosed. The letter read:

> *Greetings from the Rockies in the Springtime with the first flower that blooms—despite temperatures at night often below freezing. This furry pioneer of spring is known as the Pasque flower—an inspiration after a long winter and a sure sign it is safe to discard that itchy long red underwear.*

> *I am looking forward to the pleasant associations this summer when the welcome people from Kansas and Iowa gather to revive the social life of Gilpin— and I do mean that for positive.*

> *For some reason not quite clear to me, my entire winter was spent at the cabin, and I rather enjoyed it.*

> *My status as an old maid is now fully established—at Christmas time I was adopted by a large white cat—apparently deserted. While cats are not my favorite animal we have struck up quite an amiable relationship due in part no doubt to the fact we are both children of an isolated wilderness or a reasonable facsimile thereof.*

> *Your card and note at Christmas time was enjoyed.*

> *Best Wishes, Slater*

In the early '70's Slater began having heart problems which prevented him from returning to the high altitude of his mountain cabin. He died in May, 1972. The following summer Jo Price stopped by the cabin to give us a memento from our good friend. It is a set of diminutive tea cups and saucers from Czechoslovakia in shades of green, red, and yellow. When children come to the cabin, we have dress-up tea parties and sip drinks from those delicate cups. Slater would be pleased.

This chapter wouldn't be complete without mentioning our good friends, Ray and Glayde Lezotte. The Lezottes bought the Rollinsville grocery from Slaughenhoupt and Slaughenhoupt in 1955, and we became their regular customers—and pests. We usually stopped to say
"Hi" and buy a few groceries as we took
our daily trip to town to pick up the mail.
We depended on them for much more than
groceries, and as I look back on it now, I
wonder why they ever put up with us.
Before anyone up Lump Gulch had tele-
phones, we'd tell people to call and leave
messages at the grocery. When we gave
potential guests directions to the cabin,
we'd say, "If you can't find us, stop and
ask at Lezotte's Grocery." Ray finally got
smart and made a map which he handed to
anyone who walked into the store with a
puzzled expression. Maybe that's one

Ray and Glayde Lezotte and Betty Campbell at the Lezotte Grocery.

reason we had so much company those first few years, and why, as I read my old letters about the people who spent time with us, I often say, "Now who were they? I don't remember anyone by that name." When the Rollinsville community well was no longer available to us for our drinking water, Lezottes let us bring our jugs to fill at a faucet at the back of their store.

Instead of paying for our groceries as we bought them, we had a running account under the heading of "The Kansas School Marms," and we'd settle every couple of weeks or so. I don't remember the reason for that arrangement except that we probably didn't think far enough ahead to keep a supply of cash.

Ray was a great tease, and we never knew what odds and ends he might slip into our grocery sack when we weren't looking. It might be a bunch of onions, or some other produce that was need-
ing a home. Sometimes it was a good surprise, such as a candy bar or a piece of fruit. One day we ordered a ham hock, and when he weighed it, he was so shocked at what it was going to cost us that he slipped a box of shrimp into our sack.

The grocery store had a storeroom built into the hill at the back of the building. Because there were no windows, it was a very dark room—not a place to spend any time unless the light was on. We always liked taking our guests into the store to meet the Lezottes, and often Ray would invite them to inspect his back room. Once he had them inside, he'd walk out, switch off the light, and shut the door.

In 1965 and 1966, when the Tolbert family spent the summers at Blue Spruce, Del, the father, helped out at the store when he was needed. A strong bond developed between the two families, especially with Ray and three-year-old Sara. Sara had diabetes and had to be very careful of her diet. Whenever the Tolbert family came into the store, Ray would try to find some kind of a treat for Sara. When the things he'd offer her had to be rejected, he'd say, "Can't that kid eat anything?" The relationship was so strong that when the Lezottes died, Sara was remembered in their will.

We always got a warm greeting when we returned each spring, sometimes with welcome signs fastened to our gate entrance. One summer we returned from a trip to find this sign at our front gate: "TOTI EMUL ESTO."* Ray confessed to having made and put it there but wouldn't tell us what it meant until we had pondered it for a few days. The explanation is found at the end of the chapter.

The Lezottes cared about Rollinsville and the people they served. They did all they could to help revitalize that little community, offering their financial support and their services to anyone who was willing to make improvements. When an elderly customer wanted "just a little paint" for sprucing up her kitchen, Ray opened a new gallon and gave her the amount she needed.

When we returned home from a trip, we found this sign by our front gate. What did it mean?

When Ray and Glayde sold their grocery in the early '70's and moved to Longmont, they gave us a couple of pieces of furniture that Ray had made for his cabin up Travis Gulch. The living room coffee table and floor lamp are examples of his handiwork. They are constant reminders of a lot of fun times with a couple of mighty "friendly folks."

Margaret LeFever was Postmistress at the Rollinsville Post Office when we first started going there for our daily mail pick-up. I don't know what her span of service was in that position, but I'm guessing that it was her lifetime work, and she took it very seriously. Bill Briscoe remembered that she never missed a day, never had a substitute, and always stayed open until 5 o'clock, no matter what the weather conditions might be. She lived in the first house up Gamble Gulch, about a mile out of Rollinsville, and she walked to and from work each day. Bill would sometimes offer her a ride. He'd stop the car and be sure she knew who he was, and then he'd say, "Now get in and I'll drive you home," and she'd say, "Oh, no thanks. I'll just walk."

Margaret had lived alone in the family home in Gamble after her mother died, except for a brief time when a brother lived with her. In fact, he was living with her when he died. She walked home from work one winter afternoon, found him dead, walked back to town to make the necessary phone calls, and walked home again. This makes her sound like a tough mountain woman, and I guess she was, but you wouldn't have known it to look at her. She was short, small boned and a little fragile looking. We called her, "Little Miss LeFever."

The LeFever homestead was on the Gamble Gulch road.

We always enjoyed passing the time of day with her, and though she was quite shy, she seemed to appreciate our visits. One day when I walked into the post office, Little Miss LeFever was practically jumping up and down with excitement. "I think this is for you," she beamed, "I think I figured it out. See how it's addressed with the three circles? I think they're rings. I think it's for you." Sure enough, one of my corny friends, instead of addressing the letter to Esther Rings, had simply drawn three rings above the "General Delivery, Rollinsville, Colo." Margaret was also pleased the day I asked her to pose in front of the post office with her sister, Mrs. Slaughenhoupt, the former grocery store owner, while I took their pictures.

I never discussed theology with Little Miss LeFever, but I have a strong sense that her take on life was similar to the Celtic philosophy of finding the Holy in the ordinary. I'm guessing that her faithfulness and loyalty to her job as postmistress came out of a sense of the importance of her mission, and an assurance that she was doing the thing in life that she was supposed to be doing, that she was following her bliss. As Joseph Campbell and Bill Moyer expressed it in their book, *The Power of Myth*:

Margaret LeFever and her sister, Mrs. Slaughenhoupt, former grocery owner.

> *If you follow your bliss, you put yourself on a kind of track that has been there all the while, waiting for you, and the life that you ought to be living is the one you are living.*

Rollinsville now has a new, modern post office, and people have box numbers instead of General Delivery. Ol' Timer dwellers don't have much occasion to go to the "P.O." since we have the mail delivered to the boxes in front of the Hamilton cabin, but I'm glad that I was around when the daily mail pick-up was a part of the community social life, and that the community social life included Little Miss LeFever.

You couldn't find better friends than Alan and Nora Jaffe and their two adult children, Sara and John. They have the cabin at the edge of Snowline Lake, just up the road and around the corner from The Ol' Timer. As usual, we can thank Robert for meeting them at the mailbox when they first arrived in the gulch and getting their life history. We hadn't known them long before we claimed them as extended family. They have shared their cabin with us in many ways, bedding down our overflow company, providing showers and baths, entertaining more sing-along guests than any cabin should be expected to hold.

They stored Toho in their garage for a number of winters until Alan decided he needed it for his new purchase, an antique Lincoln Continental convertible with suicide doors. Suicide doors are back doors that opened the opposite way from standard back seat doors, and, I guess, are somewhat dangerous. When Alan first told Nora that he was going to need the garage, she was indignant. She said, "You can't have the garage. It's Toho's." That tickled me. I found other storage places for my Terrific Toyota, and we had a lot of fun riding up and down the back roads in Alan's new toy.

Alan and Nora have more friends than they can keep track of. It's possible that they have more summer company than we do at The Ol' Timer. Alan likes to show his guests what an old log cabin looks like, so he brings them down the road to our place to see the log walls, the wood-burning stoves, the wooden ice box, the pump organ and wind-up phonograph, and all the other cabin treasures.

Nora is especially close to the Hamiltons and to Florence Gooch, and she keeps in touch with them as she and Alan travel the world over. Fun, caring, generous, and thoughtful neighbors, the Jaffe family is high on our list of "forever friends."

Our adventurous friend, Florence Gooch, introduced us to her adventurous friend, Kay Russell, and together we became an unofficial high mountain adventure club. Each summer we get our heads together and plan a 'daredevil' trip or two. Sometimes we've gone in Toho, sometimes in one of Kay's more reliable 4-wheel drives, and often we've collected enough of a crowd to need two tough "mountain goats." We've explored the hills above the old town of Caribou, wriggled our way through the narrow trails leading to McClellan Pass, taken the breathtaking trip to the foot of James Peak and down the other side to St. Mary's Lake and Glacier.

Kay is one of those delightful combinations of "city lady" and "intrepid mountain woman." She and her husband Bill have apartments in Denver and Central City, as well as an elegant Victorian home up the hill from their Central City apartment. Bill was mayor of Central City for a number of years and is an authority on mining and railroad history. Kay keeps very busy entertaining opera goers, opera cast members, and friends from all over the country and around the world. She has spent endless hours supporting the local art museum, the Episcopal church, and, I'm sure, many things I'm not aware of.

Fortunately, Kay has a wonderful sense of humor, and she has needed it on a number of occasions. One that I can still picture vividly happened the day that she brought her friend, Gary Montgomery, to the cabin to witch for water. We knew we were going to have to have a new well, and we hoped that a water witch could give us a clue as to where to dig. Robert and Marj had joined Sally and me and our guests for a picnic. We had spread our food on a picnic table in the side yard—chips, dip, potato salad, hamburgers, drinks, and what-have-you—and were enjoying congenial conversation. Sally, Gary, and I were sitting on the attached benches on one side of the picnic table, and Marj,

Robert, and Kay were on the other side. I decided I needed something from the cabin, excused myself, and left the group. While I was in the cabin, the phone rang, and it was for Sally, so she excused herself. Before long, for some reason, Gary got up from his perch, and as I came to the kitchen door on my way back to the picnic table, I saw the most amazing sight. With nothing left to weigh our side of the table down, it began to rise slowly into the air like an unbalanced teeter-totter taking Marj, Robert, and Kay slowly and gracefully to the ground. There they were, the Hamiltons and Kay, lying on their backs with their seats still on the bench, their feet and legs still in sitting position, and their clothing covered with food

Robert, Marj, Sally, Gary Montgomery, and Kay Russell, before the table tipped.

and drink. Robert had chips and salsa in his armpits, and Kay was, among other things, drenched in tea. I stood immobilized until the laughter from the three told me that no one was hurt, not even their pride. I've never asked Kay if her pin-striped seersucker jacket and white pants ever came clean. I don't want to know.

On one of our trips on the McClellan Pass road above Georgetown, we met a snowdrift that stopped us in our tracks. There was no way to turn around, so the passengers got out and directed me as I inched Kay's Lexus 4-wheel drive back to a fork in the road.

The tension must have affected our bladders, and we all agreed we needed a "potty stop." There were no trees in sight, only a few scrubby bushes, but they'd have to do. Kay, who is always prepared for any kind of emergency, pulled a roll of toilet paper from the back of her vehicle, and as she started down the steep hill to find a little privacy, the roll slipped from her hand and started its own descent, leaving a ribbon of white in its path. Kay had a longer hike than she had intended, but she did retrieve it, and we all crossed our legs and had a good laugh.

Kay Russell and Nora Jaffe had an unexpected hike retrieving the toilet paper roll.

It's April 12 as I'm writing this, and just today Sally and I began our Colorado talk. Maybe I'll call Kay tomorrow to get her permission to print these stories, and I'll say, "It's time to get out your high-country map and start planning for our 2002 4-wheel drive adventure!"

*Ray Lezotte's sign "TOTI EMUL ESTO" —TO TIE MULES TO

FULLENWIDERS AND OTHER FRIENDLY FOLKS

Marj, Esther, Margaret Gooch and Marthanne Hogrefe (Florence's daughters), Kay, and Florence. We were on our way to St. Mary's Lake via James Peak. Sally was taking the picture.

Some of our high mountain adventures took us higher than the clouds.

Alan and Nora Jaffe sitting on the deck of their cabin with Snowline Lake in the background

Kay Russell, "city lady" and "intrepid mountain woman"

Marj, Esther, Robert, Sally, inspecting Alan's antique Lincoln Continental convertible with the suicide doors.

CABIN CHORES AND PROJECTS -OR- YOU CALL THIS A VACATION?

Ken definitely needed supervision when he poured the new cement stoop for the Hamilton cabin.

Ken didn't think much of my job as supervisor when he was spraying the cabin logs.

Irene is good help indoors or out. Over the years, she and Ken have hauled a lot of logs for cabin fires.

It took sons Mike and Scott to help Charley carry the cast-iron, claw-foot tub into the front yard for the yard sale.

Granny Ethyl and Jim Davis were a big help with the advertising.

CABIN CHORES AND PROJECTS -OR- YOU CALL THIS A VACATION?

Robert was good at soliciting help. Neighbor Sid Copeland and Kansas friend Glen James helped him mend the fence. Whitey said, "Take my picture."

It was hard to watch Charley standing on a sawhorse placed on top of Toho so that he could get a good swing on those large nails. When he had finished the new gatepost, we had a dedication ceremony.

Marj helped me load Toho for a trip to the dump. Good ol' Toho, and good ol' Marj.

Great-great-nephew Christian DuBois and neighbor Oliver Van Everen took it seriously when we asked them to be the percussion section for a sing-along.

Brother Clarence should have been a landscape artist. The year his family vacationed at the cabin, he spent most of his time cultivating this wild rose garden.

CABIN CHORES AND PROJECTS -OR-
YOU CALL THIS A VACATION?

Charley passed his kitchen skills on to son Scott, who made the birthday cake for his mother, Sara. Pictured: Tina and Scott James, Charley and Sally, standing behind the honored guest.

When Charley tore the linoleum, tar paper, and stacks of newspapers off the dining room floor, he found the trap door leading to a dirt cave below the dining room.

There's no "free lunch" at The Ol' Timer, not even for children. When 18-month-old great-great nephew Cole Bumen, son of Kevin and Kim, visited the cabin in 2001, he helped re-build the wall along the path to the kitchen door.

Sometimes after Sally and I have made chore assignments to all the guests, we slip off to a favorite spot for a little vacation.

RITUALS, CELEBRATIONS, CEREMONIES, AND GENERAL FOOLISHNESS

"Last year I gave myself one hundred and eight celebrations…
I cannot get by with only a few."

from *I'm In Charge of Celebrations* by Baylor and Parnall

This is a most difficult chapter. Why? Because my photo albums are chock full of pictures of special occasions: this party, that celebration, those ceremonies. All are special, but I'll share just a few. Don't look for smooth transitions from one event to another as I review these happenings. The connector is, "good times up Lump Gulch and surrounding territories."

Ol' Timer celebrations began in August of '53 when we invited the Central City gang to picnic in our newly acquired side yard. This gathering is mentioned in the first chapter, "The Adventure Begins." The next year, and for several years following, the Ye Olde Fashioned work crew and associates met at The Ol' Timer for the annual unbirthday party. We drew names and exchanged gifts and participated in a lot of harmless mischief.

Family celebrations began in '54 and have been happening every year since. It might be someone's birthday or anniversary, or if there's no legitimate occasion, we can always bring one into being. In July, 1955, we had three generations of family and friends visiting at the same time. The guest list included Mom, the Hamiltons, and their daughters, Carol and Jan. Doris and Charles Sheetz had brought her mother, Iva Shuberg, and their two children, Jay and Doris Jean, and several other couples had wandered in.

While Merrill Slater is having a sniff of spirits, Ray Lezotte is checking out Merrill's bloomer apron.

I don't remember what we were celebrating, but something prompted me to teach the group a circle dance. Whatever the occasion, you can tell from the picture that spirits were high and so were the feet. It warms my heart to see that Mom (back to camera) was participating fully. That dear saint, full of grace and wisdom, was also full of merriment.

Circle to the right, then give a big kick.

We've had a number of family reunions since that first one in 1954.

I wouldn't believe, if my photo albums didn't tell me, that we had a family gathering in 1987 and another in 1988. Two summers in a row is a lot of togetherness. The cover photo of this book, the "saps" dressed in weird costumes standing in front of the cabin, was taken at the '87 reunion when we created our own costumes and characters for a play we called "Hamiltons Revisited." It was a situation comedy, the situation being that Marj and Robert thought they were finally going to have a cabin summer all to themselves, but one by one, or two by two, the mob descended. While

Gathered for the 1987 reunion were: Bob, Lana, Esther, Jeannie, June, Sally, Marj, Carol; standing behind are Charley, Robert, Jan, and Chic. Were there only twelve?

the guests were taking over the place, the Hamiltons slung their belongings into their bags and got the heck out of there. Preacher brother Bob, the Right Reverend Robert Raymond Rings, Retired Rector, was with us, so we had our Sunday morning worship service in the cabin living room and Bob preached. We had a choir which sang "The Robin's Return," an appropriate title since our family has a round robin letter, and we often begin with, "Dear Robins." It usually takes about six months for the letters to make their rounds, but if one waits long enough, the "Robin" will return.

When the group was gathered, and before the service began, we made a presentation to niece Jeannie Bumen, brother Glen's daughter. You'll need a little background information to appreciate the gift and the poem. Jeannie likes to play the role of the "little princess," needing lots of attention and special favors. At this reunion her night nest was the top bunk in the back bedroom. She complained that it was too hard to shinny down from that lofty roost to use the pot, and she wondered if she could have a bedpan, fur-lined for warmth and comfort. I had an antique bedpan which must have been among the original cabin treasures. We painted it blue to match the bunk beds, bought a yard-sale coat with a fur collar, lined the pot with the fur, and presented the gift to Jeannie with the following poem:

Before the Sunday morning worship service we presented Jeannie with a gift and a poem.

Little Princess of the "pee," when at night you have to "wee,"
Don't descend from lofty roost where to return you need a boost.
Use instead this heirloom quaint, decked with fur and matching paint.
But when the liquid nears the top, please don't do another drop,
For soggy beds are worse by far than using yonder chamber jar.

178

Though we took up the Sunday morning collection in Old Drum, the large whiskey bottle, (Jan missed the opening and spilled about three dozen pennies onto the floor) and the choir wore bathrobes, giving the excuse that the new choir robes hadn't arrived yet, we did have a thought-provoking sermon followed by a lively discussion. The morning, with its combination of silly and serious so typical of the Rings clan gatherings, was a ritual of family bonding.

Probably the most exhausting family get-together was in 1988 when we celebrated Christmas in July, Fourth of July, and Newells' fiftieth wedding anniversary all in one long weekend. For

The choir had to wear bathrobes as the choir robes had not yet arrived.

the Christmas festivities we trimmed an evergreen tree brought in from the woods and made more fooler gifts and more original "poemtry." The gift I received was not a fooler. It was, of all things, a microwave for The Ol' Timer. It sits in the kitchen next to the wood-burning Buck's Range. It seemed pretty funny at the time, but now I don't know how we'd manage without it.

"City lady" June and husband Chic were proud of their 50th anniversary gifts of travel wear. Please note June's J.C. Penney outhouse boots.

Christmas was followed or preceded, I don't remember which, by the Newell anniversary party. While Jeannie is the "little princess," sister June was often referred to as "city lady" June, since she had more refinement than most of us. She usually hiked in dressy sandals, saying, "If I'd known we were going to hike I'd have worn something casual." "Ha, ha," we'd say. We gave June and Chic a money tree for future travels and supplied them with lovely travel outfits, including my J.C. Penney outhouse boots for June's delicate feet.

Somehow in the midst of all this celebrating, nieces Jan, Carol, Jeannie, and Sally decided they didn't like my orange and brown curtains next to the wine-colored upholstered wicker rocker. I said, "If you want them changed, you'll have to buy the material and make new ones." The words were barely out of my mouth when the four of them were collecting themselves for a trip to Boulder. If my mind serves me, which it often does not, I think they returned from town and had the curtains, as well as a few decorative pieces, finished before bedtime.

The July 4 festivities included the "you all come" invitation, and by the time the weekend had expired, so had we.

We credit brother-in-law Robert with initiating sing-alongs into our summer festivities. You may remember that a question he put to any new acquaintance was, "Do you sing or play a musical instrument?" We never knew how many people he had invited to our sing-alongs. We've had over thirty guests smushed into the cabin living room and spilling over into the dining room and bedrooms. I wish I had kept a guest book over the years. Just reading my old letters the family saved for me is a reminder of the variety of people who passed over The Ol' Timer's kitchen threshold, some I can't recall ever having met. Not all of our sing-alongs and celebrations have taken place at The Ol' Timer.

We've had rousing song-fests and celebrations at Jaffe's cabin on the lake, the Proffit's home just off the road to the old Fort Cody site, and at the Fullenwider/Vrana cabins on the Tolland road.

Not everyone could get in the picture taken at Al and Nora Jaffe's sing-along.

Ed and Evelyn Proffit, far right, didn't know we'd wear our "finery" when they invited us to High Tea.

Our ceremonies and celebrations usually involve numbers of people, but there are rituals connected with cabin life that are calm and quiet and introspective. Sally and I have rituals associated

Sessions clock, a gift from Marj, is the heartbeat of the cabin.

with our Sessions shelf clock, a treasured cabin gift. Marj brought it from Topeka in 1956, and it took its place on a shelf on the dining room wall above Grandpa Hittle's old Morris chair. It is the heartbeat of the cabin, the first thing we take from its winter hiding place each spring and the last thing we tuck away. Winding it, leveling it, starting the pendulum's sway, and listening for the first tick-tock is a ritual which signals, "Life at the cabin has begun for another summer." Sally and I have the deepest affection for Sessions, and we speak kindly to it as we open its hinged glass front, take its brass key from underneath its pendulum and wind first its ticker and then its bonger at bedtime on alternate nights.

We have a fairy slipper orchid ritual, which includes a June hike down the Brinkerhauf path. About halfway down the hill leading to Gamble Gulch, we veer to the left and begin our search for the remains of an old buckboard fence. (We don't know why it's called a buckboard fence, but that's what George Merchant called it, so we know that's what it is.) The decaying fence boards create a boggy soil that welcomes these rare and delicate orchids.

We also celebrate the wood lily, another rare mountain flower. There are so few of them left that we don't broadcast its whereabouts, but early in July we slip off to its hiding place. We search out its deep orange petals and graceful green leaves, and praise it for its beauty and its endurance. These acts of mindfulness and appreciation of nature's gifts are for us rituals of gratitude.

The Tolbert family, Mary, Del, and their four children, Cindy, Susan, Steve, and Sara, were longtime friends of Betty Campbell, and when Betty became part of the cabin scene, so did they. Del was an elementary school principal and had flexible summer schedules, so for two years, 1964 and

Sara Tolbert, age three, did not like the Sara-mony.

1965, the family spent the summers at the Blue Spruce cabins down the road from us. They were as fond of celebrations as we were, and we made special occasions almost a daily occurrence. The day we were hiking and found our first columbine of the season I said, "This calls for a ceremony." Sara, age three, began to cry. "What's the matter, Sara?" we asked. "I not Sara-mony," she sobbed, "I Sara Tolbert." After that we referred to our ceremonies as celebrations.

One day when the Tolbert family was at the cabin, a hummingbird flew into the kitchen window and suffered a fatal blow to the head. We had a burial with teenage Susan serving as the minister. We placed the tiny creature in a small container and filed into the aspen grove with shovel and solemn faces. We dug a hole and laid the poor thing to rest, and Susan gave an eloquent eulogy. Her final words of comfort were, "He was a fine bird, but a poor flyer."

Susan Tolbert is much older in this photo than she was when we buried the hummingbird.

During the summer of 1987, Robert and Marj left the cabin for a week to visit June and Chic in Oregon. While they were gone, someone suggested that we needed a mayor for our Lump Gulch community. Why not, upon the Hamilton's return, get the gang together for a potluck and elect Robert the Mayor of Gilpin? Over thirty hill folks got into the act—finding props, planning speeches, writing songs, making funny gifts—and when the Hamiltons returned from their travels, they were greeted with an invitation to a potluck at the Ball cottage. They hadn't a clue what was about to take place. After a typical neighborhood meal together, Doug Ball called the town meeting to order, and the fun began. I can't begin to describe all of the foolishness that took place at that gathering, but Vince Suich, Sr. deserved the prize for the best speech. Everyone knew that one of the instruments Robert played at sing-alongs was the violin, or fiddle. Vince's speech went something like this:

Robert "fiddles around" at our sing-alongs. Nancy Vrana is our amazing keyboard player.

I question the wisdom of electing Bob Hamilton as our chief. Do we want a mayor who's always fiddling around? Not only that, the other day I stopped for the mail and Bob came out to say, "Hello." I said, "Hey, Bob, where's your car?" He said, "It's in Nederland; it's missing a little." I said, "What do you mean, 'It's missing a little.' It looks to me like it's missing a whole lot."

That occasion was the first, last, and only time we ever saw Robert Hamilton speechless.

181

A couple of great articles about the Hamiltons, the sing-alongs, and the election appeared in *The Mountain Ear*, the local newspaper, one that summer and another in 1988. They are worth recording for posterity.

Hizzonner and Erhonor
Bob and Marg Hamilton

Erhonor Marg and Hizzonner Bob

by Bonnie Merchant

Hizzoner and Erhonor — that's Robert and Marg Hamilton of Gilpin Town.

They were elected by popular vote of the ghost town's current residents, he to be the mayor and she to keep the mayor tightly in hand. The popular couple have been close to the hearts of those who have been fortunate to know them for the 35 years they have been spending the summers in their cabin in Lump Gulch.

Both Bob and Marg have opened their hearts and their houses throughout the 50 some years of their marriage to a variety of family and friends and have carried that tradition to their summer home in the mountains. Frequently hosting and always leading the traditional summer sing-a-longs in the gulch, Bob makes them special "You all come" celebrations for the neighborhoods and their friends and guests. Everyone brings their own instruments:

an organ, a keyboard, guitars, banjos, violins, even a train whistle and a tuba have furnished the background for an enthusiastic chorus of old favorites. Singing (or a reasonable facsimile thereof) is loudly enjoyed by all, reading the words from mimeographed sheets. Homemade food is part of the evening's intermission while weary fingers rest and others catch up on the local news that is the order of the day.

Bob and Marg hold the key to the city (wooden and three feet long). Bob has a very unsteady black top hot, a bright red sash of distinction, and presides with a rubber mallet that sometimes Marg is tempted to borrow with purpose.

Hugs and happiness abound.

In the winter Bob and Marg are residents of Topeka, Kansas. Their two daughters, Carol and Jan, live in the same part of Kansas with their individual families. All

of the branches of the families are frequent visitors to Gilpin.

Long mountain hikes, care of the birds and animals, early breakfasts, late talk-a-thons, moonlight strolls, and parties given upon the slightest pretext fill the summertime hours. Marg seems to be able to conjure sleeping arrangements out of thin air. Folks from all over the United States come to stay and share the fun and reluctantly leave. Locals wander in and out as they can free their calendars for relaxation and enjoyment.

If you meet the Hamiltons on the street, you will want to stop and talk awhile, get your name on Bob's file of local folks, take a walk with Marg, and be welcomed Lump Gulch style to the festivities. Don't forget to tune up your instruments and your vocal chords before coming. It is a lot of fun.

182

aug. 11, 1988

Sing-along celebrates summer

By Barbara Lawlor

As the evening sun slowly slipped into Snowline Lake, the summer residents began to arrive at Al and Nora Jaffe's cabin. It was their turn to host the annual sing-along that has become tradition for the folks who have come and gone for as many as 35 years.

The Jaffes, who live in La Jolla, Calif., are the youngest of the group members but the activity has become a highlight of the summer for them.

There are hugs and handshakes as the old-timers greet each other. Many of them bear treats for the intermission. Bob Hamilton, the honorary mayor of the ghost town of Gilpin, brings his guitar and his wife Marjorie. Actually, he drove and she walked.

Last year, the group had presented him with an honorary key to the city. "It was the most embarrassing moment of my life," says Hamilton. "It was a railroad job. Who wants to be mayor of a ghost town?"

Central City's ex-mayor Bill Russell arrives, explaining apologetically that he is really out of practice but he'll take a stab at it.

Doug and Caroline Ball bring their talents and musical repertoire. Ball has been spending summer's at Snowline since he was 6 years old. His parents Max and Molly Ball bought the property in 1925 and formed the Colorado Fur Farm to raise silver foxes for their skins.

They named the company Snowline which would inform people that these foxes had been raised in rugged weather and therefore had grown lush coats. But the business faltered during the Depression, and the Balls sold the farm to Art Crow.

Crow eventually sold the farm, turned about 50 pairs of foxes loose and bought the Stage

MAYOR OF A GHOST TOWN—Bob and Marjory Hamilton, summer residents of the former Gilpin townsite, have been returning to their teeny cabin for 35 years. Hamilton was elected mayor last summer.
Photo by Barbera Lawlor

Stop Inn.

Snowline Fox Farm became the subdivision Snowline Estates, but once every summer, at the annual song-fest, all those years fade away and the group might just as well be back in 1943 when Doug and Caroline were married, and folks had their bets on the foxes.

After hellos and how-are-yous, Hamilton blows into an instrument announcing the beginning of the sing-a-long. Mimeographed sheets are handed out, and the first number is called.

There is still a glimmer of light shining on the lake as the aspens turn dark in silhouette. He calls out number 76, "There's a long, long trail a'winding." Nostalgic notes waft out the still-open window.

"We'll find perfect peace, Where joys never cease; Out there beneath a Western sky."

Folks who live elsewhere, from all over the country, settle down for the next few hours, sharing the songs and their lives in one special night at the end of summer.

HAMILTON FOR MAYOR
Tune: *Clementine*

In a gulch in Gilpin County
Lies a peaceful little town
Filled with ghosts from days of mining
Though much gold was never found.

Little Gilpin, little Gilpin,
Now we come from states around
To enjoy our little city
Where good fellowships abound.

What we need now is a mayor
Who will keep us all in tow;
It must be a friendly fellow
Whom each gulchman's sure to know.

We want Robert, We want Robert,
We want Robert Hamilton.
If a need in town arises
He'll be sure that it gets done.

As Mayor of Gilpin, Robert had the upper hand.

We never know what garb Ken and Irene will be wearing.

Many of the good times we've had with Ken and Irene Shaw would come under the heading of "general foolishness." We never know what kind of get-up they'll be wearing when they arrive, what noisemakers they've discovered, or what tricks they might have up their sleeves. Just having the Shaws at the cabin is cause enough for me to celebrate. I must admit, it's partly because they are such good workers. I could never have held that ancient cabin together without Ken's skills and labors and Irene's ingenuity. A more important reason to celebrate them is that they're full of fun and good humor, and we build on a storehouse of togetherness that began fifty years ago in college and just won't quit. Several years ago at a cabin breakfast, Ken noticed that we were serving him Grapenuts that had an expired date on the package. He has never let us forget it. The next year when the family arrived, he and his two grandsons were dressed as super-sleuthers, intent on catching us in the act of serving outdated cereal.

Sally and Esther watch as Steve and Shawn inspect the expiration dates on the cereal boxes.

184

The McGrath/Wiggs contingent from Nederland contributes a lot of spice to our summer smorgasbords. Linda adds such instruments as washboard, spoons, paper bags, and plastic tubes called Boom-Whackers to our sing-alongs, and Rich is proficient on a number of instruments, including the melodica. Jane and Linda both come up with "luscious" meals, our favorite being Aunt Elma's barbecued chicken. Larry upgraded our outhouse several summers ago with a new device called a

Tri-Mode Output Processor, or T-Mop, model 10001. The large box which Larry installed on an inside wall of the Gilpin Annex has a hidden bell inside, attached to a push-button T-MOP activator on top, and a movable indicator on the front to allow the user to indicate which of the three holes has been used—left, center, or right. The instructions for its use are:

POST IN A CONSPICUOUS PLACE

NOTICE

Congratulations! A Tri-Mode Output Processor (T-MOP) has been installed in this facility as a part of the endless quest for modernization. Use of the T-MOP will cause no conflicts with Privy Police or other authorities. Please read the following instructions carefully:

Operation of the T-MOP Model **10001**:
         denotes 3- holer

1. Select the appropriate output processing mode (left, center, or right) by moving the pointer lever located on the front of the T-MOP.

2. When paperwork is completed, push the T-MOP activator located on the top of the unit. More than one activation may be necessary, depending on judgement of the user.

Failure to activate the T-MOP Model 10001 after each output could result in sanctions by the Privy Police!

L&J McGrath

After the installation was completed, a ceremony was held on the steps of the Gilpin Annex, and a song written by Linda and Rich was sung to the tune of *Clementine*.

Larry installed his latest invention, the Tri-Mode Output Processor, in the Gilpin Annex.

ODE TO GRANNY'S OUTHOUSE

Verse 1:   In a cabin, down in Lump Gulch,
        Excavated for some mines,
    Lived a miner, forty-niner,
        by his privy in the pines.

Chorus: Oh, the outhouse had no flusher,
        only holes that were so deep!
    For the miner, forty-niner,
        twas a gem he had to keep.

Verse 2:   In the cabin, down in Lump Gulch,
        Granny Ethyl came to stay,
    With Esther's bathrobe, granny glasses,
        and her hair was silver gray.

Verse 3:   Oh, the Ol' Timer rocked with good times,
        many years have rolled along.
    Up the hill still stands the outhouse,
        and the Gulch is filled with song.

Verse 4:   Oh, the outhouse is so festive,
        with its skull upon the door.
    But Granny Ethyl was determined
        to upgrade it one time more!

Verse 5:   Granny Ethyl searched the catalogs
        in the country far and wide.
    Then she ordered a clever T-MOP –
        NOW SHE FLUSHES WITH GREAT PRIDE!

L&R Wiggs

At first we thought our new outputter would give us a high rating with the county commissioners, but we kept reading dire warnings in *The Mountain Ear* that, in spite of any real or imagined

upgrades, outhouses were on their way out. Therefore, we went forward with plans for the new indoor plumbing I have heretofore described. The June 29, 2000, flush was worthy of many celebrations. The first ceremony/celebration was attended by our two funny friends, Lin and Nancy Vrana. They came up the path on a Friday evening carrying their towels, soap, and shampoo, asking, "May we use your new facility?" Nancy had brought her accordion, an addition to any special occasion, and we gathered in the new bathroom to admire all of its features. As a finale we sang a variation of the song, "Please Release Me, Let Me Go."

Lin and Nancy asked, "May we use your new facilities?"

The new bathroom ceremony included the singing of "Please Relieve Me, Let Me Go."

Not all ceremonies are joyful occasions. When our friend Bill Briscoe was found dead in his Denver apartment, the hurt and sense of loss went deep. The military memorial service planned by his nephews and for the public at large was a fine tribute to Bill, with taps, the three-gun salute, the flag, and words which did justice to our friend. But his mountain friends loved the side of Bill that was gentle, warm, humorous, down-to-earth, and nature-loving. We needed to honor him in his Moon Gulch setting, keeping these qualities in mind. Bill had taken us a time or two to a spot on the ridge between Moon Gulch and the Tolland Road. It was his own Centerville mine, and it had an expansive view of the Continental Divide. This was the spot we chose for saying good-bye to Bill, this friend who had delighted us in so many ways.

The road to the mine leads through private property and then becomes practically no road at all, not a place for your average vehicle. Therefore, ten of us piled into two four-wheel drives, took our picnic food with us, and started on our journey, only to find that the gate to the private property was locked. In spite of our disappointment, we found a picnic spot on a lower road, built a bonfire, and had a wiener roast with all the trimmings. Just as we were finishing, we saw a car going up the higher road toward the locked gate. They were surely the owners of the private property, friends of Bill's. I took my long legs up that hill as fast as I could go and caught them before they had time to lock the gate again. They were delighted with our mission and let the gate swing wide. We reloaded our vehicles and made our way to the Centerville Mine. I had taped some of Bill's favorite stories, so we sat on chairs and picnic tables that either he or the property owners had provided, and we listened to his familiar voice with its Southern drawl spin yarns of people, places, and poltergeists. Then we sat quietly for a time, absorbing the view and remembering. As we were bringing our ceremony to a close, I looked up to see a large hawk circling over us. It stayed right over the Centerville Mine, and we watched as it circled higher and higher until it was out of sight. It was minutes before any of us could speak.

Robert Fulgum, in his book, *From Beginning to End: The Rituals of our Lives*, says:

> *The most powerful rites of passage are reflective—when you look back on your life again and again, paying attention to the rivers you have crossed and the gates you have opened and walked on through, the thresholds you have passed over....*
>
> *I see ritual when people sit together silently by an open fire, Remembering...*

For me, this book has been a love-feast of remembering. When I go to bed after working on one of these chapters, I close my eyes and see with clarity the people, places, and events I've been writing about. What a gift!

What a miracle!

I found a Tibetan folk story in the book *Thank You*, a collection of quotes compiled by Dan Zadra.

> *On the morning of his 50ᵗʰ birthday a prosperous merchant sprang out of bed with a grin. Singing and whistling, he saddled his favorite ox and dressed in his finest robes.*
>
> *"Where are you going so early?" inquired his wife.*
>
> *"Today I am fifty and grateful," he laughed. "Today I shall ride back down the road and thank all the ones who made such a difference in my life."*

Telling my stories has been a "going back down the road" thanking people who have made a difference in my life.

As I bring this opus to a close, I am filled with such gratitude—I am spilling over in all directions. It seems that there are some things in life that come together in such a way—with such a perfect fit—that one wonders, "Did I have any say in this, or was it part of some mysterious plan?" Such is the case with *Saps From The Pines*. This book began, developed, and is coming to a close in ways that were and are not of my doing. It has been the result of "the right people, in the right places, at the right time"—an amazing team effort. Glory, Hallelujah!!

RITUALS, CELEBRATIONS, CEREMONIES, AND GENERAL FOOLISHNESS

Those present for the T-MOP ceremony: Marj (standing left); Linda, Granny, Esther, Jane (seated); Sally, Rich, Robert; Betty Field (behind tree) Larry. Roger Field was behind the camera.

There are a number of things of import in this photo: Grandpa Hittle's old Morris chair, the new curtains the cousins made, my favorite wicker rocker held together with twine and duct tape, the lighthouse in the window, and most important, the beautiful wood floor, nephew Charley's handiwork.

Columbine and aspen cover the hillsides around the Brinkerhauf path.

Finding the delicate fairy slipper orchid is a yearly ritual.

Every summer we go in search of the wood lily, a rare mountain flower.

On the day of the memorial we held for Bill Briscoe, Kay Russell and Florence Gooch enjoyed the view of The Divide from his Centerville Mine.

189

Printed in the United States
by Baker & Taylor Publisher Services